CRUSH MOM GUILT

CRUSH MOM GUILT

TRANSFORM YOUR LIFE FROM
CRAPPY TO HAPPY
AND IGNITE YOUR INNER GREATNESS

TRINA + TARA O'BRIEN

Crush Mom Guilt © Copyright <<2023>> Power Mom LLC

All rights reserved. No part of this publication may be reproduced, distributed or transmitted in any form or by any means, including photocopying, recording, or other electronic or mechanical methods, without the prior written permission of the publisher, except in the case of brief quotations embodied in critical reviews and certain other noncommercial uses permitted by copyright law.

Although the author and publisher have made every effort to ensure that the information in this book was correct at press time, the author and publisher do not assume and hereby disclaim any liability to any party for any loss, damage, or disruption caused by errors or omissions, whether such errors or omissions result from negligence, accident, or any other cause.

Adherence to all applicable laws and regulations, including international, federal, state and local governing professional licensing, business practices, advertising, and all other aspects of doing business in the US, Canada, or any other jurisdiction, is the sole responsibility of the reader and consumer.

Neither the author nor the publisher assumes any responsibility or liability whatsoever on behalf of the consumer or reader of this material. Any perceived slight of any individual or organization is purely unintentional.

The resources in this book are provided for informational purposes only and should not be used to replace the specialized training and professional judgment of a health care or mental health care professional.

Neither the author nor the publisher can be held responsible for the use of the information provided within this book. Please always consult a trained professional before making any decision regarding treatment of yourself or others.

For more information, email powermom@powermom.co

ISBN: 979-8-88759-587-0 - paperback

ISBN: 979-8-88759-588-7 - ebook

Get Your Free Gift!

To get the best experience with this book, I've found readers who download and use the Power Mom Action Guide are able to implement ideas faster and take the next steps needed to become strong and confident . . . all without mom guilt.

Get your copy by visiting:
www.crushmomguilt.com/action

Dedication

To my wife Tara and our twins, Tristan and Teegan—
our family is my everything.
To all moms, take one step at a time. You deserve this.

Table of Contents

Chapter 1:   What's Your Why 17

Chapter 2:   You're Not Alone. 25

Chapter 3:   It's Your Time to Shine 31

Chapter 4:   Creating Your Power Mom Hour 39

Chapter 5:   What You Believe, You Receive. 47

Chapter 6:   What's Your Relationship with This?. 53

Chapter 7:   Time to Power Up 63

Chapter 8:   Green Light, Yellow Light, Red Light . . . Stop! . . . 77

Chapter 9:   A Turning Point 91

Chapter 10: Become a Power Mom Private Investigator (PI) . . 109

Chapter 11: Slay Excuses and Create Endless Motivation. 115

Chapter 12: Everything Leads to This. 129

Chapter 13: Action Takers Reap the Benefits 139

Preface

Montrose, Colorado, December 2022
Our Journey; Now It's Your Time

Bitter-cold air blanketed the house. Inside, a red-hot fire crackled inside the black wood-burning stove, keeping the house warm and cozy. Tara and I sat at our white-washed kitchen table, dinner dishes scattered on top. Our bellies were full, and our conversation light.

"How long have we known each other?" Tara asked.

"Oh gosh, I don't know," I replied

As she began clearing the kitchen table, Tara said, "Where is that picture of us? The one of us in Daytona Beach where we played in the sand soccer tournament together? It had the date on there. Was it 2002? Yes, I think so. But we knew each other well before that. I graduated college in 1996. So it had to have been around that time."

"Oh wow," I laugh. "That's twenty-six years—yikes! How did you get so old? So we've known each other for twenty-six years, have been married for fourteen, have eight-year-old twins, and we are now writing a book together. What a journey it has been!"

It's true. Our lives together have been a journey, and everything we've learned and experienced together has led us to create this book together. We are Trina and Tara O'Brien—co-founders of Power Mom. We are partners in business and in life. The main voice of this book is me, Trina, while Tara's knowledge and insights are deeply embedded throughout the book. Just a note; some names have been changed, and some stories have been modified to protect private moments and those we love and care about.

We wrote this book to empower and inspire the greatness within you. Thank you for walking this with us. In some ways, I feel like you are with me as I write, and it is my hope you will feel me with you as you read, just a friend sitting with you at a coffee shop, listening to your inner dreams and desires, and giving you hope and guidance where I can. I want to be there with you. This is for you, after all, and you deserve this.

Foreword

Mom guilt. It's the deep, dark side of motherhood that no one talks about. But it's there, and it's real. In everyday decisions, guilt seeps through the cracks of your mom-soul, and you question if you are giving, doing, and being enough. It robs you of giving time to yourself.

You were once an athlete who walked with strength and confidence. You felt larger than life. The world was yours to be had. Within your life journey, you became a mom, one of the greatest blessings on earth. And while the upsides of being a mom far outweigh the downsides, at the end of the day, the downsides weigh heavily on you.

Your body changed *a lot* when you gave birth. Now, when you look in the mirror, you are pained by your reflection, and you no longer feel strong and confident. You lack self-love. Your life is full of demanding kids, stressful work, piled-up laundry, and dirty dishes. You've put everyone and everything else first while putting your body, wants, needs, and dreams on the back burner. You struggle with exhaustion, motivation and lack of time.

Crush Mom Guilt

And it isn't all your fault. We know you've tried to make changes. But none of the fad diets and programs have worked. You're frustrated and confused, and you don't know where to turn. But deep down, that athlete mentality burns inside, and you desire to feel strong and confident again. What if I told you there's a better way and your life doesn't need to be a constant struggle?

I'll explain. Tara and I have been where you are, and we understand how you feel. After having our twins, we were suffering. Our relationship, our fitness, our emotional states, everything was in disarray. This went on for months until one day, Tara hit a wall and had a total meltdown. That was our beginning. Tara and I both played college soccer, and we are now massage therapists and health enthusiasts. Tara holds a Master's degree in Leadership, while I have a Master's degree in Sports Management. Together, we dug into our arsenal of knowledge and created Power Mom, which led us to write this book.

Within these pages, we share our personal journeys and our journey together. We've leveled up our lives and now love who we are; as individuals and as a couple. We reveal how we've gone from feeling exhausted, unmotivated, and having mom guilt, to living a life of energy, confidence, strength, and self-love.

We unwrap and empower you to move within our 4 Power Components. We give you our years of experience and break them down into simple, doable steps. At the end of each chapter, we offer you a Power Mom Action Step. We encourage you to answer the questions and create ideas and a vision with each step. Be thoughtful and specific. Get quiet, listen to your heart, and write down what inspires you from within. You will dream and love yourself again. It's all inside of you. You just need to re-spark that inner fire and let it come roaring back to life. Do this, and you will become strong and confident . . . all without mom guilt.

It's time for you to step into your power. You've already let the days, months, and years slip by. Please don't go on living this way. Now is your time to act. The past is gone. This very moment is all you have.

As one of my favorite mentors, Katherine Lee of Pure Hope Foundation, says, "The moment is over, but what you choose at that moment creates your future."

Your moment, your future, is now. So, turn the page and go create your strong and confident future self. We can't wait to see how you grow and thrive.

Chapter 1

What's Your Why

Your Home, Today's Date
Coffee, Daydreams, and Adventure

Beep. Beep. Beep. Your alarm clock crows. The day begins.

You stumble to the bathroom. Your reflection tells the tale—tired, puffy, red eyes. You pee and brush your teeth, wondering how you're going to make it through your day.

Coffee. You head downstairs and hit the beloved red button on your coffee pot. Drip, drip, drip. Ahhh, the smell of dark roast aroma.

You click on your phone and mindlessly scroll through Facebook. Five minutes pass. The dripping stops. Your head snaps up as your focus returns to the real world. You grab your favorite coffee mug, which reads "Best Mom Ever," and pour the fragrant black liquid into the cup. As you watch the steam rise, the aroma drifts into your nose. Ahhh . . . you pour in the sugar and cream, stir, and take your first sip. Mmmm . . . a sweet taste explosion.

Crush Mom Guilt

Bang. The savored moment is gone in a flash. It's time to get the kids moving. Morning craziness. Wake kids. Dress kids. Feed kids. Make lunch for kids. Grab a sip of now lukewarm coffee, two sips if you're lucky.

It's your turn. You shower and get ready. You yell to the kids, "Hurry and get into the car." Accompanied by the daily reminders, "Grab your lunch, your cleats, and don't forget your homework."

You speed off in the car, drop your kids at school—in the nick of time—and head to work. You sip on your now cold cup of coffee. The craziness of the morning sinks in. You sigh. The day has just begun, and you already feel overwhelmed and drained. You daydream about the moment you can put the kids to bed and veg out on the couch.

As you drive, you come to a stoplight at the local college. You notice two girls crossing the crosswalk. They wear matching red and gold shirts with "Bulldogs" across the back. Their names are printed on the front: Krys De and Angi. They're chatting excitedly, their bodies animated. They reach the other side of the street and head towards a group of girls all wearing matching shirts—an athletic team of sorts.

The light turns green, and you pull away. Your mind wanders to a time not so long ago but one that feels worlds away.

It was a sunny, hot day. Pre-season. As you pulled into the school parking lot, you felt butterflies in your stomach. You parked, got out of your car, and, as you did, saw your teammate Nikki getting out of her car. You walked over, and as she saw you, her face lit up. You're both excited to see each other and hug. Nikki was your best friend, and she loved the game of soccer as much as you did. You're both strong, fit, and vibrant, ready to start the next soccer season.

You remember the energy of the team that day. Electric. You could smell the fresh-cut grass and feel and see the heat rising from the ground. Your teammates were chatting excitedly about what was about to come. Sprints.

Warming up, you ran a couple of laps around the field and stretched. As the warm-up ended, your coach headed to the other end of the field. Sprints time. He called everyone over. You and your teammates headed his way, dreading what was to come.

After twenty minutes of hard-fought, out-of-breath, I-might-die moments, sprints were over. You collapsed to the ground and felt your chest rising and falling as you worked at catching your breath. Sweat rolled down your face and arms; your light gray shirt was now dark gray. You'd survived another day of sprints, and it felt good. You smiled to yourself. You felt alive, strong, confident and ready for the rest of practice. After swigging some water, you high-fived your teammates and trotted back to your coach. Time to scrimmage.

You sigh as your mind slips back into reality. You've reached the parking lot at work. As you park, you look in the rearview mirror and see your reflection. Guilt and shame flood your mind and heart as you see how much you've changed since your college days. You once had lean, toned muscles, but you now see soft muscles and fat. You wonder what has happened to you. You've tried all the diet programs—from calorie

CRUSH MOM GUILT

counting, ready-to-eat foods, food restriction, and cleanses—yet nothing works, and you're discouraged. Tears well in your eyes. You're glad you're nestled in your car, and no one can see you crying.

As you wipe away your tears and slide out of the car, you realize how much you miss your teammates and those hard days of practice. With a chuckle, you realize you miss the structure, discipline, and even sprints. You say hello to a co-worker as you step inside work, and your workday begins.

As your day continues, you can't help but shake thoughts of who you were and who you've become. You reflect on what's happened since you graduated. You found a great job, married an amazing person, settled down, and decided together to have kids. Now, life is crazy busy and coming at you a hundred miles an hour. Hours pile into days, days turn into weeks, and weeks lead to months. All that time, you meant to begin working out and eating better, but you're busy and overwhelmed and don't even know where to begin. You're sick and tired of starting something, then stopping, starting something new once more, and stopping yet again. You're embarrassed, frustrated, and lost; part of you wants to throw your hands in the air and stop even trying.

You've picked this book for a reason, and Tara and I are glad you did. We know you are seeking answers to becoming strong and confident again . . . all without mom guilt. We know this book will guide and lift you.

Which part of this mom's story resonates with you? Does it scream, "Hot damn, this is me," or, "Geez, this is definitely the

What's Your Why

story of my life?" What made you pick up this book, and why now? Hint: your first thought is most likely the real reason!

Your answer is what we call "your *why*." Your why is unique and important, and it only belongs to you. It's the compelling reason behind your motivation to continue on the journey—this adventure—we're going on together. We're going to help you dive in and develop your why more. How exciting! You may even find times in your life when your why will anchor you and keep you going, even when the going gets tough. Taking time to define your why is an important first step.

I remember a time when I had to dig deep into my why. It was a hot, sticky August morning in South Florida. College soccer pre-season was in its first week, which meant the team was doing three-a-day practices. Swimming in the morning, fitness and drills in the afternoon, and scrimmages at night. For swimming, my soccer coach hired a swim coach named Michelle. Some of my teammates, including me, called her "The Beast." With a nickname like that, you can only imagine how excited I was to start my days off under her control. Insert eye roll.

That summer was my first season with the team, and I hadn't known what to expect. I came into pre-season unfit and soon found myself a part of the "extra club"—meaning I had to do extra swimming after almost everyone else got out of the pool. This addition was hellacious. One day, The Beast told those of us in the extra club to get into the middle of the pool and tread water. So, we did. After what felt like an eternity—which was most likely only a minute—I considered sinking to the bottom of the pool and never returning to the surface. Since that wasn't a realistic option, I considered getting out of the pool and quitting. But something inside of me fought through those last few moments of doubt, and I stayed in the pool.

That day, I was happy enough to have survived. Looking back, I know *my why* kept me in that pool. Staying on the team, and becoming a starter, was more important to me than quitting. My why propelled me forward and helped me work hard to reach my goals.

It is essential to start with your why because, without it, you'll find it nearly impossible to stay focused and committed to your journey. Your why needs to be meaningful to you and deeply connected to your heart. Your first thoughts regarding your why might be your kids, spouse, or work role. These things are important.

But your why is about what you *feel within your heart and soul*; your why is something you can't deny. Something so profound it will pull you through moments of self-doubt and temptation. It will help you get back up if you've fallen down and support you in taking one step at a time.

Discovering your why may make you cry, and that's a good thing. Give yourself permission to dig deep and let your feelings and emotions come out.

Have you found yourself saying or thinking something similar to:

"I've tried so many times, *but* . . . "

"I need to work out, *but* . . . "

"I can't seem to stay or get motivated . . . "

"It's too hard to eat healthily . . . "

Excuses like these will sabotage your life and prevent you from becoming your ideal self. You need to shift your focus from excuse-making to reason-making. Let's get you moving!

Power Mom Action Step:

Write down the answers to the following four questions and add your why after each. This can be one sentence or more. Remember, this is about who you want to become. Be open and honest. This is for your eyes only, so dig deep and go big!

Example: I want to live a healthier lifestyle because I want more energy and to be active with my kids.

1. Why do you want to become strong and confident?
2. Why now?
3. What are you willing to do to become your ideal self, inside and out?
4. Why will you succeed?

When you really understand your why you can have total chaos around you, and no matter what, your why and your belief in it are so strong you will do whatever it takes to keep going.

Chapter 2

You're Not Alone

Colorado Springs, Colorado, February 2016
Tara's Defining Moment

The reality blindsided me. I was sitting in my small, cozy office when I heard my co-worker say, "Good night, Tara." I responded with a "good night" and glanced at the clock; 5:25 p.m. Ugh, time was flying by. I still had so much work to do, but I knew I needed to get home. I'd left the house for work at 6:30 a.m. without seeing my six-month-old twins. I rose, grabbed my coat, picked up my work bag, and headed out to the car.

I slid into the seat of our mommy van and inhaled the new-car smell. The cold from outside and the exhaustion of the day followed me. I put my bag inside, started the van, and felt a deep, dark reality stirring inside me. As I started to drive away, I realized I didn't want to go home. I pulled over, stopped the car, and put the car into park. I screamed at the top of my lungs and slammed my hands on the steering wheel. I broke down into tears, sobbing with anguish, anger, and frustration. Time seemed suspended while I stayed in the throes

CRUSH MOM GUILT

of emotion for several minutes. Everything around me was as dark as my thoughts and desperation.

My corporate job was demanding, and the pull between home life and work life sucked the life out of me. The thought of walking into the house and transforming into "Mom" felt daunting. It was a horrible realization, but it was how I felt. I was exhausted, overwhelmed, unmotivated, and stretched thin. I loved my kids and my wife, but I felt I was swimming upstream, day in and day out. I had no time for myself, and I'd let myself go. I'd put everyone before me, and I'd put myself on the back burner. I was slipping back into my old, unhealthy eating habits. I'd stopped bringing lunch to work and was eating out every day. Pizza, subs, chips, loaded burritos—I avoided salads as if they were the plague. My afternoon delight was a handful of candy from the candy jar at work. Each morning I'd drive by the gym right by my work and promise myself I'd call and join. I never did. I was losing myself in mom life. Long gone was the woman who'd once felt strong and confident.

I grabbed a tissue from my bag and wiped my eyes and nose. I turned on the car, pressed the gas, pulled back onto the road, and started the drive home. I reflected on a question I'd recently read, "Do you want to be average? Because average is like everybody else."

Growing up as an athlete, I'd continually strived to be anything but average. I wanted to be the best player on the soccer field. I wanted to be the best at what I did for work. The experiences in my younger years drove me to excel and be better than average. Yet, here I was, living a below-average life, and I was unhappy. I knew I needed to change—something had to change.

I pulled into our driveway, put the car in park, sat in silence, and gathered my thoughts. "Okay, I can do this," I told myself. I gathered my stuff from the car and walked into the brightly lit, warm house. Squeals of delight greeted me as the twins saw me walk in the front door. My heart melted and ached at the same time.

Trina came around the corner from the kitchen to say hello and stopped short. She could see something was wrong. "Is everything okay?" she asked.

"Yes, and no," I sighed. I set my bag down in the entryway, walked over to her, and held her in a long hug. I whispered, "Let me say hello to the kids, and then we can talk."

That night I opened up with Trina and shared what I was feeling. She listened. When I finished, she said, "You're right; something does need to change. While my circumstances are different, I, too, have been struggling. Let's find a program that can support us." That night we searched online but couldn't find anything that fit what we were looking for.

The programs we found were exclusive and only focused on one area of life. For instance, some companies focused solely on food—counting points or calories or offering specific types of foods or made-for-you meals. Other programs offered workout trainers, life coaches for personal challenges, and family support programs for the whole family. We didn't find a single inclusive program that embodied a holistic approach to all areas of life—personal, physical, nutritional, and relational.

After several days of coming up empty-handed, Trina and I decided to be proactive and create our own plan, and that is how our Power Mom VIP program was born. It's been a journey with some ups and downs, but we've gone from:

- Exhausted to energized
- Unmotivated to confident
- Feeling mom guilt to strength

We've leveled up our lives and now love who we are; as individuals and as a couple. We know the Power Mom VIP program works because we live it every day. We believe everyone has the right to be a better mom, partner, friend, leader, or whatever supports you in your best life. This book takes what took us years to perfect and breaks it down into simple, implementable steps. We've been where you are, and we know how to coach you to become who you want to be.

Our secret sauce to success is the Power Mom Daily Practice. We believe wholeheartedly in the following statement by F.M. Alexander, "People do not decide their futures, they decide their habits, and their habits decide their futures."

You are a creature of habit. For instance, you most likely brush your teeth every morning and night, right? You may or may not enjoy brushing your teeth twice a day, but you know it will keep your teeth from decaying and keep your gums healthy, so you do it.

The Power Mom Daily Practice takes this simple concept and guides you to create healthy habits within 4 Power Components:

Power Component #1 – Building You: Clarify the exact action steps you must take to reach who you want to become. We call this your 2.0 Version.

Power Component #2 – Fueling You: Learn how to keep nutrition simple without counting points or calories.

Power Component #3 – Training You: Become fit and embody real results without hours in the gym.

Power Component #4 – Extending You: Evaluate where you are today within your personal relationships. Then, develop a plan focused on strengthening and growing within these relationships.

The first three Power Mom Components focus on personal development, and in return, you'll have more to offer to those you care about and love in the fourth step.

As the daily practice becomes part of your routine, you'll create new, healthy habits. You'll condition your mind to focus on simple daily tasks that lead to daily success. These daily successes lead to weekly successes, monthly successes, and yearly successes. The key is having a simple plan that removes overwhelm and creates clarity and consistency. The Power Mom Daily Practice is a tried and proven system that is sustainable long-term.

Power Mom Action Step:

It's time for you to create your personal Power Mom Daily Practice. Answer the questions below for each Power Mom Component area. Expand as you'd like, and be as specific as you can. Be clear about your action step, time, place, tools, equipment, and so on. Make your daily actions realistic, so you can be consistent.

Building You: Choose one action that allows you time and space for yourself without interruption.
Example: I will meditate and journal the first twenty minutes of my morning in the loft before the kids wake up.

Fueling You: Choose one habit you'd like to develop around nutrition.
Example: I will eat snacks that incorporate fruit, veggies, healthy fat, and protein. I'll have two snacks a day, the first at 10:30 a.m. and the other at 3:30 p.m.

Training You: Choose one or more exercises to integrate into your workout routine. Choose something you enjoy doing.
Example: Four times a week, I will go from work to the yoga studio down the road and get my workout in.

Extending You: Choose one relationship you'd like to grow and strengthen. Envision and plan for how you will make this happen.
Example: I will spend one-on-one time a minimum of once per week with each of my kids and do a fun activity of their choice.

Chapter 3:

It's Your Time to Shine

San Francisco, California, April 2018
Trina's Push To Growth

As I step onto the hotel balcony, a cool, gentle springtime breeze blows across my face. The sun's morning rays peek over the mountaintop, illuminating a light blue sky. I walk over to the railing and notice small, green buds scattered on trees and bushes below me. I smile as I nervously think about the exciting day ahead.

An hour later, I step out of the elevator and into a bustling hotel lobby. The energy in the air is electrifying. I follow the signs that point me toward the conference center. As I round the corner, I spot a red and black sign that reads "Meeting Room A—The One Percent." A line of people waits outside the door, anxious to enter. Greetings fill the air as I step in line and wait to get inside. Upbeat music washes over us as the doors open, and we enter the spacious conference room. I find an empty seat at a table a few rows back from the stage. As I wait, I look around and watch people file into the conference room. I know every person in the room is more successful and experienced than I am. I'd taken this trip as a leap of faith and the time was now to level up and grow.

"You're the average of the five people you spend the most time with." – Jim Rohn

This truth is why I took the leap of faith that day and attended a coaching conference full of highly successful entrepreneurs. I knew it was time to push and challenge myself. It was time to grow. I knew I needed coaching and to surround myself with elevated-thinking people.

Have you ever considered the people you choose to surround yourself with? Have you ever thought it to be important? Awareness of those you're close with is essential. As you begin to make changes in your life, it will affect those you spend your time with. Often, your changes make other people feel uncomfortable. They may fear what your positive changes mean to them and your relationship.

For instance, have you ever told your best friend about your new eating habits and heard the response, "Does this mean we can't do wine Wednesdays anymore?" Or have you ever told your partner and kids that you are going to focus on eating more nutritious food, and you're met with, "Does this mean we can't have pizza Fridays anymore? Do we have to eat what you're eating?"

In these instances, their reactions are about them, not you. I'm not saying you should change your friends, leave your partner, and say goodbye to your kids. That's ridiculous! But, you may need to look at your outside influences. You may need to adjust who you spend your most time with or be prepared to have a heart-to-heart where you set some boundaries. You will need to guard your mind. Find ways to increase time with successful people living how you'd like to live. This is an imperative step on your personal growth journey.

To support our Power Mom community, Tara and I created a free Facebook group called Power Mom Nation. This community of moms is working to improve their lives, just like you. Together, we offer support and inspiration. We invite you to join us at:

https://www.facebook.com/groups/PowerMomLife

It is time to head into Power Mom Component #1 – Building You. In Chapter 1, we talked about your why. Now that you are clear on your why, it's time to create your 2.0 Version—the person you want to become. To get to your 2.0 Version, you must first be aware of where you are today.

The definition of self-awareness is "A conscious knowledge of one's own character, feelings, motives, and desires." You must understand where you are today to move closer to where you want to be. Self-assessment may be a difficult step, but it leads to greater self-awareness. It's time to explore your life with curiosity. This is an exciting step, so take heart!

Power Mom Action Step #1:
Right now, grab your journal or a piece of paper and a pen. Answer the following questions honestly. Don't judge; just get everything you feel out on paper.

Describe yourself.

- How do you look and feel?
- What do you think of yourself?
- What excuses do you make that stop you?
- How do you respond to stress—through binge eating, drinking, overdoing sugary or salty foods, yelling?
- Do you put everyone else before yourself? If so, why?

Celebrate and give yourself a high five for taking the time to reflect on those questions. How did that feel? Liberating? Yes? Great work!

Now that you've done step one—don't jump ahead until you've written out where you are today—it's time to create your 2.0 Version that defines who you want to become. To help you with this, I'd like to introduce you to my friend Sarah and her experience.

One bright, hot sunny day, Sarah decided it was the perfect day to go to the beach. She wanted to bask in the sun's warmth and smell the fresh, salty air. She grabbed her always-handy red cooler and filled it with a sandwich, snacks, and her favorite sparkling water. She put on her beloved bathing suit, a matching sunhat, and sunscreen. She walked out to the garage, scooped up her beach chair, and piled everything into the back of her yellow jeep.

As she jumped into the front seat and started the jeep, Sarah suddenly realized she didn't know which beach to go to. Did she want to stay local or go to a beach further away?

Should she head north, south, east, or west? Which roads should she take? Did she want to take the scenic route or the more direct and quickest route?

She wasn't sure. She knew her starting point was home, but she needed to figure out which beach to go to. Then, she'd be able to enter into her GPS her current location and where she wanted to go. The GPS would calculate the best route, travel distance, and approximate time of arrival. It'd also guide her along the way, ensuring she didn't get lost. The GPS wouldn't ask Sarah where she'd been or why she'd been there so long. Its only job was to get Sarah from where she was to where she wanted to go.

If Sarah never figured out which beach she wanted to go to, guess what? Without knowing where she wanted to go—if she didn't have a plan—no matter how much driving Sarah did, at the end of the day, Sarah ain't going to the beach.

How does Sarah's story relate to you? To create your 2.0 Version, you need to know where you *want* to go. Creating your 2.0 Version sets your intention—the clear vision of your desired outcome. Knowing where you want to go, and having a plan for how you will get there, is essential for your success. The only way to change your outer world is to first change your inner world. Spend time creating your 2.0 Version—think about it, feel it. The time you spend on this vision is crucial.

"Nothing gives a person inner wholeness and peace like a distinct understanding of where they are going." – Thomas Oppong

One of our VIP Power Moms, Maureen, had this to say about her 2.0 Version.

"So, I've been working and focused hard on Mo 2.0. Mindset is my biggest challenge. For the last few weeks, I feel like I have exploded. The bomb went off. I am making myself better."

Power Mom Action Step #2:
Get a pen and some paper and describe in detail your 2.0 Version. There is no wrong or right; this is for your eyes only.

Warning: Your brain is excellent at keeping you safe; it will play tricks on you. It will tell you stories that aren't true, so pay close attention to the stories that pop up while you do this. Work through the discomfort and let yourself dream. Even if you don't believe you can achieve what comes to mind, write it down. Step outside your current limiting beliefs, and let your imagination run!

Here are some questions to help you get started. Picture yourself as your 2.0 Version three months from now. Then explore the following (and more!):

- How do you feel?
- How do you walk?
- What are your kids, partner, family, and friends saying about you?
- How are you different physically, mentally, emotionally, and spiritually?
- How are you a different mom, co-worker, or wife?
- In what ways are you happier?

For example: "I am strong and confident in my mind and body. I know who I am and where I am going. I walk with my shoulders back, and my head held high. I feel good about myself when I look in the mirror. I'm a good role model to my kids. My kids, partner, and friends say I'm happier. I'm making better choices, and I like who I am. I love this journey, and I've fallen in love with this process and the Power Mom Daily Practice. I'm not afraid to step out of my comfort zone and challenge myself. I understand making mistakes is how I learn, and I will grow from those mistakes and rise above them. Whatever I set my mind to, I do it successfully. I enjoy preparing and eating healthy foods, and unhealthy foods no longer control me. I make good choices that build my body up, not break my body down. I love myself, and I give that love to others too."

I hope the example inspires or helps you as you answer the above questions. Have fun with this exercise, and remember to smile as you write your answers. As you progress in this book, you'll create the steps you'll need to begin building your 2.0 Version.

CHAPTER 4

Creating Your Power Mom Hour

Your Home, Today's Date
From Chaos to Power

In Chapter 1, you were introduced to "Chaos Mom." The mom who wakes up exhausted every morning, jonesing for a cup of joe, and who frantically runs one hundred miles an hour day in and day out. Remember her? We're going to flip that story from a "Chaos Mom" morning to a "Power Mom" morning.

You sense the glow of the dawn morning light as you wake from a deep sleep. The bed is warm, and your pillow is soft and comfortable. Your eyes flutter open. You glance at the window and see rays of sunlight and a gloriously orange sky peeking through the sides of the window shades. You glance at your watch, seeing one minute until your alarm clock goes off. You take a few moments to reflect on what you're thankful for.

You yawn, stretch, get out of bed, and head to the bathroom. You feel your mind and body waking up more and more. You feel great. You use the toilet, brush your teeth, drink some water, and smile as you look in the mirror. *Today is going to be a great day*, you say to your reflection as you pull on your workout clothes. After dressing, you reach for your phone. You scroll to the notes area, where you see the heading "Daily Declarations." You choose that note, look in the mirror, touch your heart, and repeat the typed words out loud, "I am filled with energy; I am enough; I love myself; I am worth it." One minute later, you're finished saying your daily declarations, and you head to the kitchen.

As you walk into the kitchen, you see your coffee pot sitting on the counter. You hit the beloved red button. Drip, drip, drip. Ahhh, the smell of dark roast aroma. No one else is awake. You relish in the quiet. While the coffee brews, you go into the next room and see your journal, current self-development book, and ear pods next to the plush loveseat. You grab the ear pods, open the black case, and put both pods in your ears. You pick up your phone, scroll to your favorite meditation app, and settle in. You choose a meditation under the self-mastery category. As it begins to play, you close your eyes and take in the sounds of the music and the voice guiding you. At first, thoughts of all you need to do for the day rush in. You refocus as you hear the meditation guide prompting you. "Sit comfortably with your back straight, in an upright position where you won't be disturbed. Now bring your awareness to your breath and breathe innnnnnnnnnnnnnnn and out. That's right." You loosen the restraints of your thoughts. You flow into a profound feeling of peace as you settle yourself into meditation.

Creating Your Power Mom Hour

Twenty minutes later, you open your eyes, adjusting to the morning light streaming in. You stretch as you reach for your journal. Time to write. You spend the next five minutes writing your concerns and possible solutions. You also add three things you're grateful for and your top two to three priorities for the day. In the front of your journal is a folded piece of yellow paper. You take it out and read over your goals. You realize some of these goals are being or have been met, and it's time to move on to some new goals. *I'll schedule some time tomorrow morning to do that,* you think to yourself. As you close the book, you refold the yellow paper and tuck it into the front cover.

You rise from the loveseat, grab your water bottle, and head to the workout space you've created. You sit down on your yoga mat, which is right next to a silver and black weight rack. You tune your phone to the workout of the day and hit play. Thirty sweaty minutes later, and feeling like a million bucks, you hit the shower. Time to get on with your day. This morning was worth its weight in gold.

The house is still quiet as you finish getting ready for work. You go into the kitchen and grab your favorite coffee mug. It reads "Best Mom Ever." You pour the black liquid into the cup. As you watch the steam rise, the aroma hits your nose. Ahhh. You take a sip and savor the chocolatey flavor. *It has the right amount of bitterness,* you think as you glance at the clock. Five minutes to spare. You sit, enjoy your cup of joe, and revel in the silence. Five minutes later, you rise and head to the kid's bedrooms. Time to get them up and going for the day.

How different does this Power Mom morning feel to you versus the story of the Chaos Mom? The Chaos Mom story may not reflect your exact morning routine, but if you'd prefer to have a Power Mom type of morning, you can create it for yourself. How? By implementing the Power Mom Daily Practice, you read about in Chapter 2. The Power Mom Daily Practice guides you to make healthy habits, through repetition, within the 4 Power Components.

The first Power Component is Building You. You've already begun constructing within this phase. You've established your Point A—where you are today. You've created your Point B—who you want to become, also known as your 2.0 Version.

Now, it is time to organize the action steps you need to take every day to reach your 2.0 Version. To get started, you're going to create your Power Mom Hour. This is an hour where you nourish your mind, body, and soul.

If you can, create this time and space first thing in the morning. Do this at a time when no one can interrupt you and protect it! Your whole day will be better, and doing it in the morning prevents the day's activities from derailing you. If mornings don't work for you, create this time at night. The key is finding a time you'll be consistent.

Creating a healthy boundary with everyone in your home about your Power Mom Hour is essential. Communicate that this is a private time you're creating for yourself. Ask your family to respect this time and only interrupt you if it's an emergency.

Creating Your Power Mom Hour

You may be thinking, *Yeah, right, an hour for myself? No way. I can't even go to the bathroom without one of my kids walking in on me.* If you are determined enough, you can create this time for yourself. Research shows that to be happier and more resilient, daily alone time is crucial. Below are the benefits of creating time and space for yourself.

- You reboot your brain and help it unwind.
- You improve your concentration and become more productive.
- You allow space for self-discovery and time for deep thinking.
- You increase problem-solving abilities and enhance your relationships.

Even kids need "me time." Unstructured activities, playing outside, and playing by themselves, boost their little brains. Kids also mirror what they see. Creating time for yourself will teach your kids that it is also important and okay for them to do so.

We all have the same twenty-four hours; what matters is what you do with those hours. What are the time robbers in your life? How much time can you find in your day to help you carve out your Power Mom Hour?

Here are three ideas that will help you create more time for yourself:

1. Go to bed an hour earlier so you can wake up an hour earlier. To ease into this new schedule, start by getting up ten minutes earlier than you do now. The next week, increase your wake-up time by another ten minutes. Keep adding this time each week, or sooner, until you create your Power Mom Hour morning. Doing this in increments eases you into your new schedule, eliminating overwhelm and tiredness, and helps motivate you to continue.
2. Order groceries online and have them delivered to your house. This can save you up to three hours a week. If you don't want them delivered to your home, use the store pick-up system.
3. Manage your time well, schedule what you need to do throughout your day, and stick to it. Schedule in your big rocks; the things that are the most important to get done. Your Power Mom Hour is a big rock, so schedule it and make that time non-negotiable. Then, fill in your other to-do's around your big rocks. You'll get so much done using a great time management system.

Here's what our VIP Power Mom Rachel shared about her Power Mom Hour:

"The 'me' time is the biggest factor. I feel that during that time, I am experiencing personal growth and learning life lessons. I feel more confident in the last few weeks, especially with my big 'ah-ha' moment. I threw away my old clothes

Creating Your Power Mom Hour

and started to make a whole different wardrobe. I feel more empowered and confident."

Power Mom Action Step:

Create your Power Mom Hour. Here are some activities that may help you get started.

- Enjoy a cup of coffee or tea in silence
- Deep breathing or meditation
- Gardening
- Listening to soothing music
- Journaling
- Praying
- Reading or listening to an audiobook
- Going for a walk
- Working out
- Doing a hobby you love, such as drawing, writing, photography, or sewing
- Yoga or Pilates
- Diffuse essential oils
- Create a vision board
- Plan your top two to three priorities for the day and plan when you'll do them—this is one action step we have our VIP Power Moms do every day.

Here are some ideas for structuring your Power Mom Hour:

1. Organize your hour by minutes and assign an activity to each section. For instance, fifteen minutes for

meditation, five minutes to journal, ten minutes to read, and thirty minutes to work out and stretch.

2. Organize each weekday with a topic or workout you want to do or focus on. For instance:

- Monday weights
- Tuesday yoga
- Wednesday weights
- Thursday run
- Friday weights
- Saturday biking
- Sunday off

There's no right or wrong way to create your Power Mom Hour. Do what works for you. The most important element is creating time for your Power Mom Hour. Next, you need to put the steps into motion. We invite you to share what you've created in our Power Mom Nation Facebook group. We'd love to know what your Power Mom Hour looks like. You'll inspire others, and we're there to help you if you need it. Use this group to support your growth through accountability.

CHAPTER 5

What You Believe, You Receive

Colorado Springs, Colorado, April 2022
Trina's Aha Moment

I looked out my bedroom window and saw the world coming alive right before my eyes. The sun glistened brightly. Birds sang and flittered by. Once barren branches were now budding with life. The brittle, dry, brown grasses of winter were now brilliant green. Springtime. So magical, wise in timing, and a symbol of new beginnings. The sight and thought put a pep in my step.

I grabbed a pair of old, worn-out workout pants and a tee shirt and got dressed. I put on my favorite baseball hat, inscribed with Breckenridge along the front, and headed out the door. I squinted as I stepped into the sun and started walking to the barn. In the cool, fresh air, I heard the crunch of my steps as I moved across the gravel.

The familiar screech of the barn door shattered the morning silence as I slid the door open. Sunlight lit up the space behind the door. My eyes adjusted as I stepped inside. I moved to the yard stuff and picked up the weed eater. I noticed it needed some gas, so I gently set it down and picked up the half-full gas can. Fumes filled my nose as I topped off the weed eater with gas and screwed the cap back on. I checked the string trimmer line and went back outside.

The grass was tall along the fence that divided the lawn from the hay fields. I set the weed eater down, inserted earbuds into my ears, and took out my phone. I scrolled to the audiobook I was currently listening to, *Looking for Lovely* by Annie F. Downs. I flipped it on, and immediately Annie's voice filled my ears. For the next forty-five minutes, I listened to Annie flawlessly weaving stories, wisdom, and words of bravery together. Her voice, and her writing, lifted me up and carried me gently away like a boat on calm waters.

Suddenly, a burning question flashed into my mind, evoking a surge of emotional curiosity. *What are you supposed to be doing but you're not doing?*

In a blink of an eye, I heard myself answer; *You need to write a book.*

A shockwave raced through my mind. Wait. What? Who, me? As unexpected as this revelation was, it felt right and familiar. I knew it was something I needed to do. For a few weeks, I kept this thought to myself. Then, one night, as Tara and I sat around the table talking, everything fell into place. She shared some things that were on her mind about Power Mom and adding a book to the mix made sense. So, I told her about my experience and that I wanted to write this book.

For the next several weeks, I thoughtfully considered the idea. While it made sense to me, it also felt massive and scary. In my mind's eye, I pictured this journey as if I were standing at the edge of the Grand Canyon, waiting to jump off and free-fall through the sky. An experience, by the way, I have no desire to have. I knew writing this book would be an adventure and would be exhilarating and challenging from start to finish.

While I felt a mixed bag of emotions, I knew in my heart writing a book was something I was supposed to do. But doubt filled my mind and robbed me of confidence. I realized I needed to work on my mental game. I knew the only way I could change my outer world, in this case, writing a book, was to first change my inner world. Whatever results and experiences I would have—good or bad, positive or negative—would reflect what was going on in my head. It was that simple. So I went to work.

Years ago, I learned about the power of declarations, so I turned to this tool to help me. What is a declaration? It's a positive statement you say emphatically out loud while holding your hand over your heart. Doing this allows each declaration's unique vibrational frequency to be felt within your body. Not only does the declaration send a clear message to the universe, but it also sends a powerful message to your subconscious mind. The combination of your hand on your heart and saying your words aloud is crucial. These two acts embody the old saying, "What you hear, you forget. What you see, you remember. What you do, you understand."

So, this is what I did. I created a list of powerful declarations. I put them in the notes section of my phone. Every morning, I looked in the mirror, placed my hand on my heart, and recited each line I'd chosen. When it came to the last declaration, I'd point an index finger to my head and state, "I'm a Power Mom." Like the magical, wise-in-timing energy of nature, I could feel my belief and confidence grow. Even now, as I write this book, I still stay true to this practice. Confidence is a muscle we must grow, develop and nurture. Declarations help.

Power Mom Action Step:

It's time to build more confidence in yourself and create your daily declarations. You can write them on a piece of paper and put them somewhere you will see them daily, or you can add them to your notes on your phone as I do. The critical step is putting them somewhere you can quickly and consistently read them.

Now, write out the declarations you'd like to recite to yourself every day. Here are five ideas:

1. I am enough
2. I am powerful
3. I am energetic
4. I am confident
5. I love, respect, and believe in myself

Inside your Power Mom Action Guide, you'll find an additional fifteen declarations, so be sure to check those out too.

WHAT YOU BELIEVE, YOU RECEIVE

If you still need to download your Power Mom Action Guide, you can do so at:
https://www.crushmomguilt.com/action

Once you've chosen your declarations, create the habit of saying these daily. Follow these steps.

1. Find a mirror to look into, put your hand on your heart, and say your declarations out loud.
2. After your last declaration, point your finger at your head and state, "I am a Power Mom."

Do this daily, and you will rewire your brain. Every thought you think creates your future. Start each day with positivity and watch your life and your belief in yourself blossom and unfold. Have fun with this, and feel free to share your declarations in our Power Mom Nation Facebook group.

CHAPTER 6

What's Your Relationship with This?

Colorado Springs, Colorado, May 2019
Trina's Night Out

The room is quiet as I step wearily inside and close the door. I notice a small, simple bathroom on my left. To the right is a large oak desk with a black and blue ergonomic desk chair. *A perfect space to do some work*, I think as I walk past it and over to a light gray couch crowded with dark gray throw pillows. I set my silver backpack and black suitcase down and take in the rest of the room. Two nightstands nestle against a spacious bed covered with a white duvet and white pillows. A pleasant mountain landscape picture hangs over the bed. To the right is a small kitchen with a microwave, refrigerator, and sink. The glowing green lights of the black microwave clock catch my eye—5:30. Great, enough time to unpack, shower, and head to dinner.

Forty-five minutes later, I walk out of the hotel lobby and into the cool evening. I zip up my light orange jacket, turn left

Crush Mom Guilt

out of the hotel parking lot, and head down the sidewalk. A quarter of a mile ahead is a busy street lined with restaurants. I pick up my pace, walking briskly. When I get to the busy street, I push the yellow crosswalk button and wait. Cars zip by as I check my Apple Watch. Right on time, I think as I see the crosswalk sign signaling me to proceed. I step into the crosswalk and head to the other side of the road. As I near the other side, I see some of my former college teammates gathering in front of the restaurant. The weariness of my travels slips away as a surge of excitement and happiness hits my heart. I turn into the parking lot and hear, "There she is!" Many smiles, hugs, and laughs later, we're seated at the dinner table. It's lined with white plates, forks, knives, and clear glasses of ice water.

My stomach grumbles as I read through the robust menu—small bites, soups, salads, entrees, pastas, and wood-fired pizzas. The Mediterranean salad catches my eye, as do the crab cakes. I close my menu and set it alongside my plate. I contentedly listen to the chatter of my friends as each discusses what they're going to order.

I hear Sally say, "Oh man, everything looks so good. Ugh. This is so hard because according to my points, I should only have a small salad. Oh my gosh! Look at the Peanut Butter Explosion dessert. Yummy, and yes, please!"

Interested, I pick up my menu and turn to the dessert page. Three desserts down, I find the Peanut Butter Explosion. The description reads, "Chocolate candy bar bottom with peanut butter ganache and chocolate mousse."

WHAT'S YOUR RELATIONSHIP WITH THIS?

As I set my menu back down, I glance up to see Jennifer and Amy looking at the menu together. Jennifer looks like a kid in the candy store as she blurts out, "My eating coach is going to kill me. But I am definitely getting the wood fire deluxe pizza. I'm certain it is going to taste much better than the frozen one my program sent me last week."

Amy nods in agreement as I hear her reply, "I'm sure your coach will understand. I mean, it's only once in a blue moon you get together with old teammates. Besides, you aren't alone. I'm supposed to be fasting right now. But I'm going to enjoy this moment and work on getting back into a routine—hopefully, tomorrow."

I turn to my right and see Beth reach down into her purse and take out a white bottle. I notice the front of the label says "Weight Loss" in big red letters. Beth quietly takes a white pill out, pops it into her mouth, and rinses it down with ice water. She quickly glances around and picks her menu back up.

A movement behind Beth catches my attention, and I see a waiter approaching our table. He reaches inside his white apron and pulls out his black pen and a white pad of paper. He asks us if we are ready to order, and Sally replies, "Yes! I haven't eaten all day. I've been saving up for this meal, and I'm starving. Hey girls, how about we start with the onion rings and loaded nachos?" Grunts of feigned guilt and "Ooohhhs" of delight fill the air. Our waiter takes note of the appetizer order, adds our drink orders, and walks away.

55

Crush Mom Guilt

Our drinks and appetizers arrive, and we fill our small plates with food. In pure leader form, Amy grabs her wine, lifts it into the air, and says, "Let's make our team toast."

We grab our glasses, raise them in the air, and chant in unison. "Here's to the nights we'll never remember with the friends we'll never forget. Cheers, big ears!" We laugh as we clink our glasses together.

I take a sip and then set my glass down. I hear Amy telling Jennifer how busy she has been with her new position as vice president of a shoe company. "I love the work. I love my team, but seriously, my life is going one hundred miles an hour. I don't have time for anything except work and attending Amanda's high school volleyball games. Thank heavens she has a great group of girls she hangs out with."

Jennifer says, "That is good to hear. She's such a cute girl. I love seeing the pictures you post of you guys together on Facebook."

"I post those pictures so her grandparents can see what she is up to. She loves taking pictures with me, but I can't stand it. I've gained so much weight, and it isn't easy to hide my second chin anymore," Amy says with a nervous laugh.

Jennifer replies, "You're being too hard on yourself! But I understand. I get out of taking pictures by volunteering to be the one to take them. I don't even like to see myself in a mirror, let alone a picture."

"Last week, I decided I needed to try another diet. I've tried so many things, but I'm going to give this intermittent fasting a go. We'll see," says Amy laughing. "I saw a friend of mine post before and after pictures, and she looks amazing. So, I figure I'm busy enough to keep myself occupied and not think about food, so why not?"

"Well, you know how I can't stand to cook. So, I decided to start one of these diet plans where they send me food. It's going ok—I guess. The kids like to give me a hard time about it. They keep telling me I should go take a healthy food cooking class or something. I haven't noticed much of a change yet. I do *love* my cheat days, though," Jennifer laughs.

Beth chimes in, "I've gained twenty pounds since my divorce. Ugh, I hate it. Things have been so hard. I went into survival mode, and I put everyone before me. I've let myself go. I've wanted to get back into exercising, but I'm always so tired by the time I get home. Once I put the kids to bed, all I want to do is veg out on the couch. I definitely don't have the energy I used to."

Sally jumps in with, "Yeah, I miss our soccer days. It was so fun and easy to go out and play! Now, for the life of me, I can't get myself to do anything. It's like I have a huge mental block or something. I try to get back on schedule, but it isn't good enough. I do so little compared to when I was fit, and it's discouraging. But I am doing a food program with a coach where I count my calories. I hope it helps, but sometimes it gets old, counting my food all the time. All I seem to think about is numbers and food. I even had a dream about it the other night!"

"I'm right there with you, Sally," says Amy. "I miss being fit and feeling good, but I do not have the time. At least with intermittent fasting, I don't have to think about food."

"Speaking of food, what do you guys think of these loaded nachos? I'm loving this salsa!" I say.

"Fantastic," says Sally as she scoops up another cheesy bite.

"I've forgotten how good this place is. I need to come here more often. I'll bring Amanda here after her next volleyball game," adds Amy.

Our dinners arrive, and we spend the next thirty minutes catching up on what is happening in our lives. The Mediterranean salad I ordered was delicious, and the crab cake was delectable. I was happy, satisfied, and full. As the busser clears our dinner plates away, the waiter appears and asks if we've saved room for dessert.

There's a silent pause; then Sally exclaims, "I've been waiting all night for this. Can I please get the Peanut Butter Explosion?"

Jennifer pipes in with, "Wow, that sounds amazing! You're speaking my language, Sally. Does anyone want to share with me so I don't feel so guilty about ordering one?"

Amy gushes, "I'm in Jenn. I mean, we've already ruined our diets. What's one more dessert going to hurt."

Beth perks up and orders the coconut cream pie. I decline to order dessert, but as I do, I ask, "Hey Sally, can I taste a bit of your Peanut Butter Explosion? I'm full, but I'd love to taste yours."

"Of course," replies Sally.

What's Your Relationship with This?

Our waters are refilled as the desserts arrive. I taste the Peanut Butter Explosion; it's sweet and very rich. Two bites and I'm good. Jennifer, Amy, and Sally are in peanut butter dessert euphoria. Beth expresses ecstasy with each creamy coconut bite. We soon get the check, pay it, and head to the door.

The evening air is cooler than before as the sun is beginning to set. I pull on my jacket and zip it up. Sally offers me a ride back to the hotel, but I decline. It's beautiful out, and I want to soak up the evening air and move my body. "Hey, when are we going to do this again, ladies?" asks Amy.

"I know, this has been *so* much fun," replies Jennifer. "We need to do this more often. We may need to go to a different restaurant, though. I'm going to feel guilty for days with all the food we ate. You were right, Sally; the Peanut Butter Explosion was to die for!"

"Oh gosh, yes, it was!" Sally exclaims. "I think we should meet up here again. The ambiance is fun, and the food is amazing. Did you see the three-layered chocolate cake the man at the table next to us ordered?"

Beth exclaims, "I did. It looked like a million yummy calories piled on top of each other." Everyone laughs. We say our goodbyes, give hugs and promise to do this again soon.

I start walking back to the hotel. My heart is warm, and my face carries a huge smile. It had been such a fun, refreshing night. I walk back across the crosswalk, reflecting on the conversations. I smile at the mom stories we shared. From kid stuff

Crush Mom Guilt

to work challenges, laundry, and dirty dishes, we were all living crazy, busy mom lives.

I enter the hotel lobby and head to the elevator. As I wait for one of the three white elevator doors to open, I hear my phone go off. I look down and see a text from Sally. It reads, "Hey, it was so good to see you tonight. I wanted to drive you to your hotel because I want to talk to you about something. I was uncomfortable bringing it up in front of all the girls. I know you are busy and have a lot on your plate, but do you have some time to talk? If not, I understand. Let me know."

I put my phone back in my pocket as one of the elevator doors opened. I step inside and hit the glowing button for the sixth-floor. The doors close, and the elevator begins to move. A few moments later, I step out into the sixth-floor hallway. I walk to my room, open the door, set my bag down, and take my phone back out of my pocket. I reopen the text from Sally and write, "It's always so great to see you, Sally. I always have time for you. Do you have some time to talk now? If so, give me a call."

A minute later, my phone rings. It's Sally. I answer and immediately hear the anguish in her voice. "Thank you for making time for me. I need a friend right now, and I know you're someone I trust and can help me."

Over the next hour, Sally shares how miserable she's been. Her life feels out of control. Every day she pretends she's fine, but deep down, she feels like she is dying. When she looks in the mirror, she feels shame and embarrassment. Where she once had lean, toned muscles, she now sees soft muscles and fat. She's been living this way for a long time. The days are piling up, turning into years, and nothing is improving. She has tried so many times to start exercising again, but after a few weeks, she stops. She doesn't even understand why. She has tried dieting, but nothing works, and calorie counting for the rest of her life feels daunting. She knows it doesn't help that she sneaks snacks every night. She intends to have one potato chip. A whole bag later, her belly feels somewhat full, but her heart and soul are heavy with guilt. She asks me how I live a healthy, energetic life, even while being a busy mom.

I say, "Sally, thank you for sharing and being so vulnerable. I know this is not easy, and I'm sorry life has been so challenging for you. Let me tell you, there is no magic pill. It takes work, focus, and dedication, but you can do it. Food isn't the enemy. Food is fuel. The key is which foods you choose to eat. You have that athletic fire inside of you. You haven't tapped into it yet, and I can coach you to do so. You can create the life you want. You can become who it is you are meant to be. I'm going to send you a link to book a coaching call with me. It will change your life."

Sally, feeling relieved, eagerly agrees and says goodbye. It's late, so I shower, jump into bed and turn out the light. Tomorrow is going to be a busy day. I'm excited to meet all the moms who are coming to our Power Mom VIP conference.

Have you had a dining experience like this before? Did one or more of these moms have a story you can relate to? We live in a "quick-fix, just diet" culture, so if you can relate to these stories, I promise that what you're feeling and what you've tried and failed at before is not your fault. Now, it is time to move forward. Over the next few chapters, you'll learn how to create a healthy and empowering mindset around food. But first, you need to create awareness around your habits and beliefs about food and dieting.

Power Mom Action Step:

It's time to get your pen and paper out again and do another self-assessment exploring your mental and emotional relationship with food.

These five questions will help you get started.

1. Which story or stories brought back memories or triggered an emotional response? What did you feel or think about it?
2. What have you tried in the past, and why hasn't it worked?
3. Do you see food as fuel or as the enemy?
4. Do you hide what you eat? Do you binge eat?
5. Do you constantly think and stress about food?

As always, write what flows out of you, be honest, and don't judge. As you explore these questions, you'll gain new insights and make space to learn how to have a healthy relationship with food.

CHAPTER 7

Time to Power Up

Boca Raton, Florida, September 1998
Tara's College Years

Beep. Beep. Beep. I wake with a start. Groggily, I reach over and turn off the alarm clock. The clock's red numbers show 10:00. Looking out the window, I see the Florida sun streaming through with promise for another hot, humid day.

I throw off the gray comforter and roll out of bed. As I step onto the cool tile floor, I feel a tweak of pain rush through my right calf. I instantly fall and grab my calf, crying out. My calf is rock-hard and feels about the size of a baseball. I squeeze it, but I feel no relief. Wriggling in pain, I scoot across the floor to the sliding glass door that leads to the balcony. I reach up, unlock the door, and slide it open. Warm, humid air engulfs me as I crawl onto the concrete slab. In front of me is a gray table with four black chairs. I grab the closest chair and pull myself up. Tears of pain roll down my cheeks as I rub my calf. After what seems like an eternity, my calf finally releases, and the pain stops.

CRUSH MOM GUILT

I lean back, close my eyes, and inhale deeply. I hear birds chirping and hear the mid-morning traffic as cars and trucks roar by on the street below. The sun is hot against my skin. I realize that my calf cramps happen more often and are getting worse. *It may be time to say something to my trainer*, I think, as I carefully get up and head back inside my apartment.

The cool air from the air conditioner greets me. I glance at my clock and see it is 10:18. I need to get a move-on so I'm not late for chemistry. I quickly shower and get ready. I grab my book bag, check my soccer bag to make sure all of my soccer gear is in there, and race out the door. The chemistry building is a short walk through campus. As I walk into the classroom, I hear my teacher asking everyone to take out their books.

Chemistry class ends, and I head out the classroom door and head across campus to the athletic building. The air is intense, and the heat and humidity are rising. My body glistens with sweat, and I still feel a slight ache in my right calf. As I turn the corner, I see the large white and blue athletic building standing in the distance. I make my way through the parking lot and see my teammate Karen parking her silver Honda civic. I walk over to her car as she gets out and grabs her soccer bag. Smiling, we say our hello's and begin walking to the building together. She notices I have a slight limp and asks if I'm okay. I tell her about my calf episode. She offers to rub some pain relief balm on my calf as soon as we get into the locker room. I willingly agree.

We enter the spacious locker room adorned with red and blue lockers. The room is bustling with laughter and conversation from my teammates. Across the room, I see my blue locker with a shiny number 7 on the front. I head over to it, greeting my teammates as I do. I open my locker door, put my soccer and book bag inside, and then sit down on the bench in front of my locker. As I do, I see Karen stride across the locker room with a yellow and blue container in her right hand.

As she approaches, I say, "Thanks so much for doing this. I hope it helps."

"Of course. I know it helps me when I'm feeling sore." Karen says as she kneels in front of me.

She unscrews the cap and scoops up a small bit of the balm. She rubs it in between her hands and reaches for my right leg. I extend my leg with anticipation and hope. As Karen's hands touch my calf, I feel an excruciatingly sharp pain shoot through my calf. I instantly fall forward, sliding from the bench to the floor—nearly landing on Karen. Whimpering, I writhe in pain. I pull my right knee to my chest, clenching my calf with both hands. Tears flood down my cheeks, and I squeeze my eyes closed, trying to push the pain away. I sense footsteps approaching and hear several of my teammates asking me if I'm okay. A hush falls over the locker room. I feel a hand touch my shoulder. Karen says, "Tara, I'm so sorry. Are you okay? Do you need us to get the trainer?"

Gritting my teeth, I mumble, "Just give me a moment." I hear my teammate Sue say she'll go and get one of our athletic trainers.

Slowly, the pain subsides. I open my eyes and see several of my teammates standing around me. I roll up into a sitting position, holding my right calf. I tell everyone I'm okay, and my teammates return to getting ready for practice.

A few minutes later, Tracy, our head athletic trainer, enters the locker room. I explain the morning's events at home and what just happened. Tracy takes a few minutes to evaluate my calf and then clears me to practice. She suggests I get treatment after practice. She knows we have a big game tomorrow, and she wants to be proactive.

By the end of practice, I'm exhausted. The day's heat and humidity have taken a toll on me. My calf pain lingered throughout practice, but I was spared another cramping episode.

I go back into the athletic building and head straight to the brightly lit athletic training room. A blue and white Florida Atlantic University logo with the words "Sports Medicine" is painted on the wall in front of me. Seven blue treatment tables line both sides of the room. Carts full of supplies stand between each treatment table. To my far left is an open door leading into another, smaller room. I hobble towards the open door. Tracy's inside next to one of the whirlpool tubs. "You ready?" she asks, glancing up at me.

I roll my eyes and reply, "Oh yeah, I'm excited about this ice bath." She laughs and tells me to get in.

I sit down on the chair next to the whirlpool tub and remove my cleats and socks. I get up and slide onto the seat of the whirlpool tub, then put my legs into the water. I instantly feel the sting of the ice-cold water. I begin taking short, shallow breaths as the shock from the cold takes over.

"Take some deep breaths, Tara," Tracy encourages. *Easy for you to say*, I think, as I watch her set the timer.

Fifteen long minutes later, it's time to get out of the ice bath. My legs are cold, but they feel better. I grab the white towel Tracy left me, swing my legs out, and dry off. Barefoot, I head back into the training room. I jump up on the closest blue treatment table, my legs dangling in front. Tracy comes over and asks how it was.

I reply, "Of course, it hurt for the first few minutes, but I feel good now." Tracy asks me to slide back as she pulls out a white bottle of ointment. She squeezes the clear salve onto her hand, grabs my right calf, and begins to massage. The pain is still there, but thankfully, I don't cramp back up. A few minutes later, she finishes and hands me two small Dixie cups. She instructs me to take them home, fill them with water and put them in the freezer. Then, before bed, take the Dixie cups out of the freezer and rub the ice on my calf. I agree and grab my belongings.

"See you tomorrow for the big game," Tracy yells as I head out the door.

As I walk back across campus, I decide I want Mexican food for dinner. I jump into my car and head to the local fast food joint. I order two bean and cheese burritos, cheese nachos, one chicken chalupa, and a diet coke. I scarf down my food, drive home, and prepare for bed.

Crush Mom Guilt

The following day I wake up feeling anxious and excited about tonight's game. We're playing our biggest rival in our new soccer stadium. My former coach, and mentor, will be at the game. I know I need to have a great game. I typically love playing nighttime soccer games when the temperatures are cooler. I feel more energized, the big lights and crowds electrifying. But as thrilled as I am, I can tell my body isn't feeling great. I'm tired, sluggish, and feel heavy. I head out the door, hoping I'll feel better as the day goes on.

As I walk through campus, heading to the math building, the intensity of the day's heat grows. I make it through my math class and then head back to the training room for more treatment.

My calf still feels sore, and I'm not looking forward to treatment. Tracy greets me cheerfully and gets started on my therapy. Ninety painful minutes later, after icing, stim, stretching, and a massage, I head back to my apartment to get my car. It's time to meet up with some teammates at my favorite pizza joint, conveniently located at the beach.

I pull into the parking lot and see the green rooftop with big red letters on the front shouting "Pizza." Several of my teammates sit at a black metal table just below a lit-up red sign that blinks "Pizza and Subs. We Deliver." I get out of the car and shuffle over to the table.

I hear my teammate Sam telling a joke. "Did you hear about the new restaurant called Karma?" After a quiet pause from everyone, she delivers the punchline. "There's no menu. You get what you deserve." The girls bust out laughing.

As I walk up, Karen asks, "Hey there, Tara, how's the calf?"

I reply, "It's okay. Tracy just tortured me with treatment for the past hour and a half. I hope it helps for tonight's game." The girls agree.

Just then, the waitress arrives with menus. I feel my belly rumble. I haven't eaten all day; I'm hungry, and I feel like I could eat my arms off. Everything on the menu looks amazing. We order a round of drinks; I request a diet coke. As we wait for our drinks to arrive, we dive into a conversation about tonight's game and a beach party happening this coming weekend. Our drinks arrive, and everyone orders food. I get a large pizza and twelve chicken wings—'cause I can't say no to that yummy mess of goodness. Forty minutes and a hundred napkins later, my belly is so full it feels like it may burst. We pay our bills and then head back to our cars.

As I walk onto the soccer field, a surge of excitement rushes through my veins. The night air is warm and heavy with humidity. I smell the recently cut grass and notice the newly painted white lines outlining the field. Two goals, one on each end of the field, stand prominently. The song "Pump up the Jam" blasts from the speakers. People are filing into the stadium and filling seats in the stands. The other team, wearing black and gold jerseys, is already on the field warming up.

A few of my teammates are warming up on the opposite end of the field from the opposing team. We're all wearing white uniforms with red numbers on our backs. I head over to my team's bench and set down my red and blue soccer bag. I double-check my shoelaces, grab a soccer ball, and head out

Crush Mom Guilt

onto the field. My calf still feels sore, but I put it out of my mind as I start to warm up.

Game time. As I head to the center of the field, I look up into the stands and see my old coach sitting three rows from the bottom. I wave as I get ready for the referee to blow his whistle. The game begins.

In the first half of the game, I'm pumped up and play well. I make the right runs and have a few great shots on goal, but the score remains zero to zero at the half. During halftime, Tracy comes over and asks how my calf is feeling. I tell her it's okay, a bit sore, but holding up so far. She hands me a bag of ice and tells me to use it.

The second half begins. For the first ten minutes, I feel great. But as the game goes on, I become tired and sluggish. I'm not making as many runs as I did in the first half of the game, but I keep pushing.

Then it happens. I see my teammate Kara dribbling the ball up the right side of the field. I'm twenty-five yards ahead of her, in the middle of the field. As she crosses the halfway line, I yell for her to play the ball into the open space in front of her. I begin making a diagonal run into that space right as she kicks the ball forward. As I do, a searing pain stabs my right calf. I immediately drop to the ground, shriek, and grab my calf. I shut my eyes tightly as if to block the pain and roll my body into a tight ball.

Moments later, the referee blows her whistle to stop the play, and I hear footsteps around me. My teammates call Tracy, urging her to come to my rescue. My teammate Julie grabs my right foot, lifts it into the air, and begins stretching it. The pain is still intense. Tracy jogs up, takes my leg from Julie, and continues the stretching. A minute later, the pain begins to subside. I slowly get up, and Tracy helps me walk off the field.

I sit down just outside of the field, along the sideline. Tracy stretches and massages my calf. My coach looks over worriedly and asks if I'm okay. With me out, we're playing one woman down. I tell him I'm ready to go back into the game. Tracy shrugs and nods her head to indicate I'm ready. I head over to the center line and wait for the head referee to wave me back onto the field.

Twenty minutes remain in the game. I do my best to get the ball and take shots on goal. But my shots are off target, my first touch off, and the ache in my calf persists. When the center referee blows her whistle, signaling the end of the game, I'm disappointed. I know I didn't play my best. The game ends in a zero-to-zero tie.

Flash forward eight years. It's 7:55 on a bright, warm, and sunny morning. I park my silver Prius in front of the downtown conference center in West Palm Beach, Florida and head inside. The cold air hits me as I walk through the doors and into the spacious hallway. I look to my right and see a sign that reads "Dr. David Phillips." This is what I've come for, and I'm excited.

I walk down the hallway and up to a white table; a pretty young woman sits behind it. She asks my name, checks me in, and I head inside the large conference room. The buzz of voices in the room is lively and full of excitement. I choose a chair right off the center aisle, fifteen rows back from center stage. I want to have a clear shot of the speaker. Dr. David Phillips is a former All-American swimmer who specializes in Sports Medicine. A friend told me about him and invited me to hear him speak.

A moment later, a young man comes onto the stage, grabs the mic, and welcomes everyone. As he does, a hush falls over the crowd as people scramble to their seats. His voice is calm yet enthusiastic as he introduces Dr. Phillips. "Dr. David Phillips graduated in 1984 from Harvard University, where he earned academic honors and was an All-American swimmer. He received his medical degree from Wright State University School of Medicine in Dayton, Ohio. After practicing as an emergency room physician, Dr. Phillips shifted his focus to sports medicine. He has competed individually in national and international triathlons, including the 2005 Ford Ironman World Championships, and qualified as a member of Team USA at the 2008 International Triathlon Union World Championships in Vancouver."

Dr. Phillips walks onto the stage, shakes the young man's hand, and takes the microphone. Dr. Phillips is tall with a lean, athletic body. He's an attractive man with blond, wavy hair, which he wears slightly longer in the back. He's casually dressed in a blue button-down shirt, khaki pants, and brown oxfords. His voice is gentle yet powerful. Over the next ninety minutes, my mind is blown. His perspectives on the crucial role of nutrition in athletic performance are eye-opening. When he's finished, he receives a roaring, standing ovation.

As I head out to my car, I reflect on what I learned. So much of what happened to me physically during my college soccer career begins to add up. I realize I didn't treat my body well, which manifested as cramping and energy problems while playing. I didn't drink nearly enough water to support my body, causing my athletic performance to suffer. The foods I consumed lacked nutrition, and I would have been healthier if I'd chosen nutrient-dense foods. I didn't know, nor understand at that time, that food is fuel. I could have done so much more to support my body; I just didn't know better.

While the story above is about how I struggled physically during my college years, I now understand the importance of treating my body properly in everyday life too. As you progress in the book, you'll find simple, easy-to-follow steps to help you learn what took me years to learn.

It's important to note your personal health journey has no destination. Yes, you'll gain new habits, new perspectives, and new desires and goals, yet personal growth is never-ending. This is one major reason we at Power Mom don't talk about or show before and after pictures. After what? There is no after. Instead, a continuation of progression and growth.

One major mistake I made was drinking too little water. Did you know water is a *secret weapon* in getting results and feeling great quickly? Check out the content of water percentages for different parts of the body put out by USGS.gov.

CRUSH MOM GUILT

- Brain 75%
- Blood 83%
- Skin 80%
- Heart 79%
- Bones 22%
- Muscles 75%
- Liver 85%
- Kidneys 83%

Cool right? In college, my go-to beverage was Diet Coke—not water. Given that my muscles consist of 75 percent water, it's no wonder I had chronic calf problems.

According to sciencenotes.org, water supports your body in the following ways:

- Main component of most cells
- Necessary for growth and reproduction
- Aids digestion
- Helps deliver oxygen
- Regulates body temperature
- Acts as a shock absorber
- Lubricates joints
- Keeps membranes moist
- Flushes body waste
- Used to make hormones and neurotransmitters

Feeling thirsty? You're already mildly dehydrated. If you ever feel or suffer from the following symptoms, increase your water intake—it could make a difference!

- Hunger between meals
- Dry mouth
- Constipation
- Deep fatigue
- Trouble focusing
- Muscle cramps
- Headaches
- Dark-colored, strong-smelling urine

Severe cases of dehydration can contribute to the following:

- Blood clots
- Infectious diseases
- Kidney stones
- Severe constipation
- Rapid heartbeat

Okay, now that we have all the water facts behind us, you may be wondering whether you're drinking enough water. Here's an easy rule to follow; take your current body weight, divide it by two, and that is the minimum amount of water in ounces to drink every day. So, if you weigh one-hundred-fifty pounds, drink a minimum of seventy-five ounces a day.

Is drinking enough water a challenge for you? If so, here are some great tips to get you started.

- Drink eight to sixteen ounces every morning when you first wake up.
- Get a water bottle you enjoy drinking from. Make sure it is easy to grab so you can take it wherever you go. You have your phone with you at all times, right? Make sure your water bottle is with you at all times too!
- Set an alarm on your phone or with an app to remind you to drink throughout the day.
- Ditch your soda habit and drink water instead. Jazz up your water with fruit, cucumbers, and herbs like basil and mint.
- Find sparkling water you enjoy.
- Drink a glass of water before each meal.

Power Mom Action Step:
1. Figure out how much water you need to drink every day. Remember to divide your body weight by two, and you'll get the minimum amount of water in ounces to drink daily.
2. If you don't already have an easy-to-grab-and-go water bottle you love, get one!
3. Choose at least two of the above tips to support you, and then implement your plan.

CHAPTER 8

Green Light, Yellow Light, Red Light . . . Stop!

Phoenix, Arizona, June 2021
Tedx Try-out Video, Food Fun

Tara: "Stop!"

Trina: "Who me?"

Tara: "Yes, You."

Trina: "Wait, what?"

Tara: "That's a *red light*!"

Trina: Whipping my head side to side, looking around, I exclaim, "A red light? I don't see any red lights around here. We're not even driving! Tara, are you going crazy?"

Tara: "I might be a little crazy, but I'm not talking about a *red stoplight*. I'm talking about that donut you're about to put into your mouth."

Trina: Looking down at the chocolate-covered donut in her hand, "What do you mean?"

Tara: "Let me tell you. Red means stop, yellow means slow, and green means *go*."

77

Crush Mom Guilt

Trina: "I'm not sure I understand. Tell me more."

Tara: "Ok. Up to now, you've been told to cut calories, eat low-fat, avoid carbs, and stay away from dairy. No, wait, dairy's not bad; your bones need it. You've been told to eat meat; it's a great source of protein. No, wait, don't eat meat; it's bad for you. It's all rather confusing, isn't it?"

Trina: Nodding her head yes, she says, "You can say that again."

Tara: "I'm going to help simplify foods and remove the confusion. Here is what I mean by red-light, yellow-light, and green-light when it comes to food. Green-light foods are foods you want to eat plenty of. These foods fuel your body and build your body up. Yellow-light foods are foods you want to slow down on and not overeat, such as low-fat, refined, and processed foods. Red-light foods are foods you want to stop eating because they are so low on the nutritional scale, including deep fried foods, foods high in sugar or artificial colors and flavors."

Trina: "So you're saying I should put this donut down because it is a red-light food?"

Tara: "Maybe. But this isn't about being perfect. Red-light, yellow-light, and green-light is a guideline to help you answer the question, 'Is this food I'm eating building my body up or breaking my body down?' After you've answered that question, you can decide whether eating what is in front of you is worth it. It helps create awareness of your food so you can make conscious decisions about what to put in your mouth."

Nutrition, nutrition, nutrition. The key is to keep it simple. Simplicity creates clarity. Clarity makes way for action. Society has criminalized food. But food is powerful and should be used for fuel. Keep this simple red-light, yellow-light, and green-light concept in mind as you move forward. Be patient with yourself as you begin to change how you eat.

- The first step is knowing what to do.
- The second step is making a plan that will work for you.
- The third, and most important step, is to work on your plan consistently; consistent implementation, over time, equals *big* results.

Colorado Springs, Colorado, May 2019
Knowing What to Do

It was a warm day, and the sun shone brightly through my office window. I was sitting at my desk with my MacBook Air laptop in front of me. I had just logged in to Zoom and was waiting for a woman named Kim to join the meeting. I'd recently met Kim at a party hosted by a mutual friend. Kim walked up to me, introduced herself, and told me she'd heard Tara and I worked with moms to help them get healthier. I said that was true and chatted with her for a bit, then invited her to set up a time for us to talk more. I wanted to get to know more about her and some of her challenges and goals. Right on time, Kim came online with her video.

"Hello, can you hear me?" She asked in a shaky voice.

"Hey!" I replied. "Yes, I can see and hear you. It is so great to see you again. How has your morning been going?"

"Busy!" she said with a sigh. "I just got back from dropping my two kids off at school and running into the grocery store. My mornings are always hectic. Sorry if you hear my son in the background sometimes."

Kim's brown hair was pulled back in a tight ponytail, and she wore an oversized black sweatshirt. Behind her were several different family photos hanging on a light gray wall.

"Not a problem. We're both busy moms, and mornings can be crazy. Tell me about your family, Kim."

"I have three kids. My oldest son is ten, my daughter is seven, and my youngest son, who is home with me right now, is eighteen months old."

"Wow! What fun ages. I can see why you are so busy."

"Yeah. I feel like I go one hundred miles an hour. I'm lucky if I get to sit down and eat lunch during the day. We're pretty good at eating dinner together unless we're running to one of my son's baseball practices or my daughter's soccer practices. We usually stop for fast food on those days. Thankfully, that is only a few times a week. But yeah, I'm so busy I really don't have a lot of time during the day to eat. But lord knows I don't need to eat more food anyways, so it doesn't bother me."

"Tell me more."

"Well, this is one of the reasons I thought I'd talk to you. I'd like to lose about thirty pounds. I've been trying to, but I haven't found any diet that works for me. So, right now, I'm just cutting out how much I eat during the day, cutting carbs and limiting my calories."

Interested and curious, I probed further. "How do you feel throughout the day? For instance, what is your energy like, and do you feel hungry during the day?"

Kim laughed, "I'm always tired, but I figure that's just what being a mom is all about. And as for feeling hungry, I'm so busy I guess I just don't notice. Sometimes I'll eat my son's leftovers from lunch, and I make my other two kids an after-school snack every day, so sometimes, I'll grab a bit of what I give them. Usually, some cheesy crackers, some graham crackers, or something quick and easy like that. By dinner time, I am usually starving. That's definitely when I eat my biggest meal. I figure that's ok since by that time, I haven't eaten much, and I've kept my calories down."

"What would you think if I told you to eat more during the day instead of less? And your problem isn't that you are eating, but what you are eating?"

"Do I have to buy pre-made foods or something like that? I really don't like packaged food or feeling like I have to be limited to a certain diet," Kim said defiantly.

With a warm smile on my face, I said, "No, you don't have to buy anything pre-made, and this definitely does not mean you have to stick to specific foods or a certain diet. Let me explain. Based on the little you've shared with me, you're eating foods low on the nutritional scale. This means foods that don't have a lot of nutrition in them. These foods don't build your body up; they break your body down.

CRUSH MOM GUILT

"I heard you mention you're cutting out carbs. I hear this often, making me wonder if carbs are misunderstood. I'll keep this easy to understand. Some carbs are bad for you and should be limited or removed from your diet. Yet, some carbs are good for you and exactly what your body needs to have long-sustaining energy. In reality, there are two types of carbs."

I went on to explain how carbs work. The two types of carbohydrates are simple carbs and complex carbs.

Simple carbs are quickly digested, low in fiber and nutrients, and high in added sugar. Limit consumption of these carbs because they don't have a lot to offer. We consider these as red-light foods. They're found in foods such as:

- Soda and other sweetened beverages
- Candy and ice cream
- Pastries, cupcakes, and baked goods
- Refined bread and white pasta
- Sports drinks

Complex carbs take more time to break down. This allows for a slower, more gradual release of energy. They are higher in fiber and nutrients such as vitamins, minerals, and phytonutrients—plant-based chemicals. They also provide energy in the form of good-for-you calories. These are green-light foods.

- Vegetables of any kind
- Legumes, including kidney beans, white beans, black beans, pinto beans, edamame, chickpeas, and lentils

- Whole grains, including amaranth, buckwheat, bulgar, farro, millet, oats, quinoa, and wild rice

After explaining simple and complex carbs, I continued, "It's also worth mentioning the importance of fiber. When I was young, I remember visiting my aunt one summer. At the time, she was doing some type of diet, and she was focused on her fiber intake. Every morning, she'd take out a container filled with a light brown powder, put two scoops of the powder in a clear glass of water and chug it down. I knew she didn't enjoy the experience, as she'd squinch up her eyes and make a funny face as she drank the drink as fast as she could."

Kim, laughing, said, "Oh my gosh. I remember my dad doing the same thing! I think his doctor told him to take it cause he was constipated all the time. Now that I think of it, my dad never did like eating vegetables. He was okay with some fruits, though."

I smiled and said, "Too funny. I think my aunt took it to help her feel full longer, which is why she drank it before she ate her breakfast." If your dad and my aunt had increased their fiber intake through food, they wouldn't have had to chug down that darn drink!"

We both laughed, and I followed up with, "That's part of the problem. Our bodies need fruits and vegetables to help with regularity and to feel fuller longer. Fiber really only comes from plants—whole grains, beans, fruit, and vegetables. Some foods high in soluble fiber are black beans, avocados, figs, broccoli, brussels sprouts, sweet potatoes, pear, kidney beans, nectarines, carrots, apples, apricots, and oats."

I pause as I see Kim soaking it all in. A few moments of silence ensued. I was eager to hear what she was thinking. She finally broke the silence and asked, "You mentioned fruit. Based on what you told me about simple carbs, doesn't fruit fall into that category? I've learned that fruit is full of sugar and really isn't good for you. But you also mentioned fruit as a good source of fiber. This makes my head spin. I'm confused! Should I be, or shouldn't I be eating fruit?"

"This is such a great question, Kim. It is true that fruit is sweet and does have naturally occurring sugar. The fiber in fruit helps slow down the breakdown of sugar in your body. Your body metabolizes fruit sugar differently than processed or added sugars. So, fruit is great for your body. Fruit contains a combination of vitamins, minerals, fiber, phytochemicals, and water that is good for you. I like to put it this way; I've never met anyone who got fat from eating too many bananas."

I chuckled and continued, saying, "Stick with the bulk of your diet being green-light foods. A colorful array of vegetables, fruits, legumes, and whole grains. Do this, and your body will respond positively. When you give your body the nutrients it needs to function optimally, it will get the nutrition it needs without overeating, and your cells will begin to replace themselves with healthy cells built with great nutrition. You'll gain energy, get healthier, lose some inches, and increase your confidence too."

"Thanks. This is really helping me out."

"Good! I know it is easy to reach for processed foods, such as the crackers and gram crackers you mentioned. These are definitely yellow- or red-light foods. Companies spend millions of dollars researching how to convince you to crave more of these types of foods. Processed foods have been engineered to reward the brain and overpower the reward from natural foods. Because of this, our brain keeps telling us to eat more, and boy, do we ever! Processed foods taste great but are high in refined carbohydrates, sugar, and artificial ingredients. They are extremely low in nutrients and fiber. They're also linked to numerous diseases and can have devastating effects on your weight."

Kim sighed and said, "So much of this is beginning to make sense. I have a couple more questions for you. How important is protein, and do our bodies really need fat? I mean, I feel fat, so I don't even want to touch anything that will add to my weight."

I grinned. "You are full of great questions, and I get these questions often. So, you aren't alone. Here's how to think of protein and fats in simple terms. First, protein is a building block for muscles, bones, cartilage, and skin. It also builds and repairs tissue. It helps carry oxygen throughout your body by way of red blood cells. Protein keeps you feeling full longer and burns more calories during digestion. About half of the protein you eat goes into making enzymes, which help with digestion, resulting in new cells and body chemicals. And you know what? When you eat protein with fiber, you'll stay full longer. This means you won't feel the urge to eat as often. As you know, the most popular protein sources are chicken, beef, and eggs. But there are also healthful plant-based sources for your protein, such as edamame, lentils, chickpeas, peanuts, almonds, quinoa, chia seeds, beans, kale, spinach, alfalfa sprouts, asparagus, broccoli, collard greens, oats, cottage cheese, and potatoes.

"As for fats, I understand the misconception. The term 'fat' in foods has been given a bad rap. Many fats are actually good for you and critical for your health. Companies and their marketing have taken advantage of these misconceptions. Take a walk down any aisle in your local supermarket, and you'll see fat-free desserts, low-fat biscuits, and calorie-counted ready meals. But while your shopping basket is bursting with these 'guilt-free foods,' the opposite seems to be happening to your waistline. Most low-fat or fat-free foods have sugar and chemicals to compensate for the loss in taste. So, *stay away!*

"Consuming healthy fats, ironically, does not by itself make you fat. You *need* fat, just the good kind. Good fats come from avocados, coconut oil, olives, fish, nuts, and eggs. These healthy fats support a healthy brain, healthy eye function, a healthy nervous system, and a healthy waistline and allow your body to use the vitamins in your food. All that sounds pretty good, right?"

Kim replied, "You know, I didn't realize how important eating real food is. I definitely need to make this a priority. Can you help me figure out some healthy snacks for my kids and me? It sounds like I need to give them healthier options than cheesy crackers and graham crackers."

Green Light, Yellow Light, Red Light... Stop!

"This is one of my favorite tips to give, Kim. There are so many fun, vibrant and tasty treats you can make and enjoy. Not only are they good for you, but they are healthy too. I have a whole list of healthy snack ideas to send you, which I'll do at the end of this call. But to give you a couple of quick ideas, have some fruit with a handful of nuts. An apple with peanut butter, almond butter, or any nut butter. Or a plate full of veggies, hummus, and guacamole that's easy and fun to dip and eat.

"I know you feel that cutting back on the amount of food you eat is good for you, but it isn't. You want to fuel your body often with healthy foods. I'm sure you make sure your car has plenty of gas to drive you from place to place. Well, you can think of food as the fuel that helps you keep your energy up and your body going."

"That sounds intimidating to me," said Kim. "I hear what you're saying, but it doesn't feel right. Ever since I was a little girl, I'd heard my mom tell me not to overeat. I get the car analogy, but I do lose some weight when I don't eat as much or as often. Those results are one reason I keep track of the calories I eat."

"How many calories are you shooting for each day?"

"Usually between 1,000 or 1,200. One of the diets I did awhile back taught me how to figure out points with calories, so I sort of follow that method to keep track."

"How has this method worked for you?"

"Well, sometimes I do a great job of following it, but it takes a lot of time and energy." Kim laughed anxiously and said, "I don't love it, but I guess it works okay, sometimes."

"You're definitely not the only person that I've heard of this method. I hate to ruffle your feathers, but the truth is, while many fad diets do recommend restricting your calorie intake to around 1,000–1,200 calories per day, it's not enough for most healthy adults."

"What? Really? Wow!"

I nodded my head, understanding her surprise and said, "Think about what we just covered. Not all foods, and therefore not all calories, are created equal. One cup of grapes is sixty calories. Three Oreos are one-hundred-sixty calories! So counting your calories may work at first, but it doesn't paint a true picture of what is going into your body. Besides, do you really want to live your life counting points and calories every day?"

No, not really," Kim sighed.

"I'm sure you don't. Cutting your calorie intake too drastically increases your risk of nutritional deficiencies. It makes your body go into survival mode. When you don't eat enough of the right foods, instead of burning fat, your body grabs onto any calories it can and keeps hold of them. Your metabolism slows down. You run out of energy. You turn to caffeine to try and get energy. Your body doesn't know what to do, so it holds on. And you're on a never-ending roller coaster ride, and you can't seem to get off. Am I right?"

"Yeah. So, what do I need to do?"

"Look, I've covered a lot with you in a short time. Stick to adding green-light foods to every meal and snack. Eat throughout the day. Set these intentions for yourself and take note of how you feel. We can set up a time to connect again and go from there."

Just before we hung up, Kim said, "Sounds good. Thank you again for taking the time to talk with me."

Power Mom Action Step:
1. Start using the red-light, yellow-light, and green-light guideline. It is a simple and fun way to teach your kids about healthy foods too!
2. Check out the healthy snack list inside your Power Mom Action Guide. If you still need to download your Power Mom Action Guide, you can do so at: https://www.crushmomguilt.com/action

CHAPTER 9

A Turning Point

West Palm Beach, Florida, March 2004
Trina's Nightmare And New Reality

It started out as a typical day, but then things turned horrible. I woke, got ready for work, and headed out the door. I pulled up to work at 7:59, quickly trotted across the parking lot, and hurried into the vast office building.

As I stepped through the front door, I saw rows of gray cubicles in front of me. To my left was a long hallway. I headed down the hallway, cheerfully greeting my co-workers. A few moments later, I entered the spacious kitchen with a fridge, five round tables, and a half-full coffee pot sitting on the laminate counter.

I opened the fridge and found a place to stash my lunch. After closing the fridge, I walked over to the counter and poured a cup of coffee. I added creamer and four scoops of sugar into my coffee, then headed out of the kitchen, back down the hallway, and into the sea of gray cubicles. I arrived at my desk, sat down and glanced out the large windows overlooking the heavy traffic of I-95 in West Palm Beach, Florida. Traffic seemed a bit busier than usual—most likely from the spring break crowd. I sipped my coffee and settled in to get to work.

A few hours later, I felt a hand on my shoulder. I turned to my left, looked up, and saw my friend and colleague, Dr. Robert Lawrence, standing beside me. He said hello and then quietly added, "I've noticed that lump on your neck. You should have it checked out."

As I watched him walk away, my left hand reached up and touched the left side of my neck. I could feel the lump, about palm size, under the warmth of my skin. It had started out as a small bump. The lump never hurt, so at first, I thought it was a knot in my neck. But the knot never went away, and the swelling increased in size over the recent weeks. I'd been ignoring the growth. The advice caught me off-guard, but the words cut through me like a knife. He wasn't telling me for just any reason; he was kindly prompting me. That afternoon, I booked an appointment with a doctor.

A week later, I walked into the doctor's office. The waiting room was small and cozy. The receptionist asked my name; I told her, and she asked me to take a seat until one of the nurses called me back. I chose a magazine from a small table in the middle of the room and took a seat. About ten minutes later, a door on the opposite side of the room opened. A young woman wearing green scrubs called my name and asked me to come on back. I followed her through the door and down the hall. We stopped at a tall black-and-white scale in a small alcove. Next to the scale was a chair. The nurse asked me to take off my shoes, put my bag on the chair, and step onto the scale. I did as asked, and the nurse moved the poised weight along the weight beam until she got an accurate read. She wrote down my weight on a white piece of paper with my name at the top and asked me to follow her to the next room.

Inside was a vinyl-topped tan medical table with a chair beside it. Adjacent was a doctor's stool tucked under a white countertop with a shiny, silver sink. The nurse asked me to sit on the medical table and let me know the doctor would be in momentarily. I waited for a few minutes, and then the doctor came in.

He was tall, thin, and had brown curly hair. After introducing himself, he started asking me about my health. How was I sleeping? I told him my sleep was okay, but I'd been having night sweats. Had I lost any weight? Yes, I answered, but I had just started a healthy lifestyle program at work, so I attributed it to that. After a few more questions, he put on some gloves and looked at my neck. Within a few moments, he told me he was going to order a test for my thyroid and would see me back in a couple of weeks. He walked me to the front of the office and left me with the receptionist to set up my follow-up appointment.

Two weeks later, after having a test on my thyroid, I went back to the doctor. A nurse called me back, took my weight, and showed me back to another small examination room. The medical table was dark brown this time, but the rest of the room was the same as the other I'd been in previously. After a few minutes of waiting, the doctor appeared and said hello. He took my file, opened it, and silently read what was inside. I heard him whisper, "Oh, no," under his breath. He looked up at me as his eyes grew big and said, "We need to do further testing immediately. This doesn't have anything to do with your thyroid. This time, we need to do a biopsy of the lump."

The next couple of weeks were a whirlwind. I'd gone to a nearby surgery center and had the biopsy done. My memory of that day was limited to being rolled into the surgery room and waking up in the recovery room. Afterwards, I was left with a three-inch incision on the left side of my neck.

The days following were numbing. As I walked back into the surgery center to discuss the results with the surgeon, I felt confused and lost. I didn't know what to expect. My girlfriend, Meg, was by my side as we were shown into a frigid-feeling room with white walls, white and gray tile, white countertops and cabinets. Even the medical table was white.

I was up on the medical table when the surgeon walked in with my file in her hands. Her manner was cold and matter-of-fact. The only words I remember were, "You need to find an oncologist immediately." The biopsy showed that I had Hodgkin's lymphoma. Cancer.

I don't remember much about the car ride home. I do remember walking into the house, falling face down onto my bed, and sobbing. I was terrified. I was also lost. I was only thirty years old. How could this be happening to me? Why was life taking life away from me? I let my best friend Jody and my family know the diagnosis. My mom wanted me to fly out to Salt Lake to get treatment. But I didn't want to leave my work, my life. Meg and Jody helped me find a highly reputable oncologist in West Palm Beach and set up an appointment.

It was now late April 2004. Jody, Meg, and I drove to the Good Samaritan Medical Center. The large window-filled building was located off Flagler Drive in West Palm Beach, Florida, overlooking the intercoastal waterway. The day was gorgeous. Blue skies, white clouds, the temperature in the high seventies, the water calm and quiet.

We walked across the parking lot, stepped inside the building, and were greeted by a young man who directed us to the elevator and up one level. When the elevator doors opened up to level one, we stepped directly inside a waiting room. To our right was a large window looking out over the intercoastal, the blue water glistening brightly. To our left was a large spacious room full of blue and brown waiting chairs. We walked deeper into the room and saw a gold receptionist sign on a warm orange-colored wall. Just below the sign was a desk where a middle-aged woman sat.

To the side of the receptionist's desk were gold name plaques recognizing all the doctors working in the oncology department. I noticed Dr. Neal Rothschild's name as we walked up to the desk. The receptionist greeted us and spoke quietly, asking for my name, ID, and insurance card. After checking in, the three of us took seats and waited. We sat quietly, taking in the surroundings. A large fish tank full of small, colorful fish sat in the middle of the room. Beautiful pictures of colorful fish adorned the light brown walls. A small gift shop full of wigs, colorful head dressings, gifts, and flowers was located just to the right of the receptionist.

A door, just to the left of the name plaques, opened and a young nurse in white appeared. I heard her call out my name, "Trina Williams." A bit dazed, I got up, as did Meg and Jody. We walked towards and through the open door. The nurse said hello and gave us a tour. To our left were scheduling, billing, and medical records. To our right were the nurse's area and examination rooms.

The nurse waved her name badge over a small device on the hallway wall. We heard a click and the two large, beige doors on our right opened automatically. In front of us was a wide hallway. Medical equipment lined the hall, as did closed doors leading to numerous examination rooms. Small green and red lights were over the examination room doors. The air was cold, and an antiseptic medical scent filled our nostrils.

To our left was the nurse's area. Just inside the opening, to the left, was a comfy-looking, green medical chair. Along the same wall was a long desk with two computers, two phones, a file organizer, and sprawled paperwork. To the right was a medical scale alongside waiting room chairs. Medical equipment of all types was located throughout the room.

The nurse asked me to step onto the scale, and after taking my weight, she invited me to sit in the green chair. Jody sat in the chair next to the scale while Meg stood beside me. The nurse, on a medical stool, rolled up in front of me and put on medical gloves. She took my pulse, listened to my heart, then turned up the shirt sleeve on my left arm. She opened a drawer to her left and pulled out a tourniquet, some needles, vials, a vial holder, an alcohol swab, a bandaid, a medical wrap, and gauze. She organized and put everything together, then gently took my arm and rotated it so my elbow was pointing down, exposing veins on the inside of my arm. She carefully pushed on one of my blue veins, put on the tourniquet, and cleaned the area of my vein with the alcohol swab.

I closed my eyes and turned my head away as she gently inserted the needle into my skin, penetrating my vein. I braved a look as she filled several vials of blood. When she was done, she placed a piece of gauze over the punctured skin, put a bandaid on, and wrapped the area with medical wrap. Everyone was quiet, taking in each moment, each new experience. The nurse stood up, grabbed my file, and walked out of the nurse's area, asking us to follow her. She stepped across the hall and into an examination room directly from the nurse's station.

We followed her inside. The room was cold, lit by bright fluorescent lights, which bounced off light gray walls. A hint of Pinesol filled our noses. Directly in front of us was a gray medical table with a streak of white paper down the middle. Above the table was a sea-scape picture. Two guest chairs were tucked in the far-right corner. A doctor's chair was pushed up against the front wall. We quietly followed the nurse inside. I sat on the medical table while Jody and Meg sat in the two chairs. The nurse let us know Dr. Rothschild would be in with us soon. Over the next several minutes, we quietly spoke about what we'd seen and wondered aloud what my future might look like.

The door opened quietly, and in walked Dr. Rothschild, dressed in dark trousers, a white button-down shirt with a striped tie, and a doctor's coat. He was tall and broad, with black, wavy hair—short in the front and a bit longer in the back. His large hands cradled an open file. His brown dress shoes made a faint shuffling sound as he stepped inside the room. Over his shoulder, I noticed a pleasant-looking, middle-aged woman following in behind him. She was nicely dressed and also wore a white doctor's coat.

Dr. Rothschild said hello and introduced himself and his physician's assistant, Mary. His voice was strong but calm and caring. Over the next forty-five minutes, he reviewed my file and test results. He answered our questions and then laid out my care plan.

The first step was installing a port. The device, a flexible tube, would be placed into a vein in my chest, just below the center of my right collarbone. The port would allow easy access for taking my blood, giving IV fluids, and receiving my "chemo cocktail"—a fancy name for chemotherapy medications. Once the port was in place, I would receive chemotherapy every two weeks for a total of six rounds. After the chemo sequence was completed, I would receive fifteen radiation treatments.

In May 2004, my port was installed. As with the biopsy appointment, I only remember being rolled into the surgery room and waking up in the recovery room. This time when I woke, I had a circular bump under the surface of my skin, just below my right clavicle.

The days leading up to my first chemotherapy were surreal. I kept my diagnosis limited to only a small group of friends. I felt their love and support. At work, I turned to my boss, VP of Sales, Tod Van Eyken. He was kind and supportive. I asked him to keep my diagnosis private for as long as possible. He was understanding and discrete. Using the plan from Dr. Rothschild, Tod and I agreed that going to chemo every other Friday afternoon would limit how much work I missed and give me weekends to recover.

One of the questions I asked the nurse during my first visit was how long it would take for my hair to fall out. The nurse had bluntly replied, "You might as well go shave your head now." It was brutally honest and hard to hear. I had long hair and wasn't ready to shave my head, so I cut my hair short instead. I hated it.

When work colleagues asked why I'd cut my hair, I'd attempt failed humor and replied, "I got in a fight with the scissors, and the scissors won." Those days were the first of many I'd spend feeling miserable, ugly, embarrassed, angry, and scared.

Day one of chemo. I went to work just as I would any other day. At noon, Meg came to pick me up. She'd told her boss what was happening, and she thoughtfully agreed to support the time Meg needed from work to help me. The hospital was only fifteen minutes away. It was another beautiful day. Warm, but not hot, the sun shining brightly, the intercoastal

Crush Mom Guilt

waters inviting. We parked and were again met by the young man at the front entrance. We took the elevator up one level and stepped out into the waiting room. As we walked down the short hall, I noticed a side of the room I hadn't before. To my left was an area of blue and brown chairs. Several people, most of them bald, sat in the area in front of two large beige doors. A wave of nervousness and anxiety washed over me. I signed in, showed proof of insurance, signed some papers, then sat and waited to be called back.

The nurse I'd seen previously opened the door just to the left of the name plaques and called me back. Meg and I followed. This time, instead of turning right into the nurse's station, we turned left into the scheduling, billing, and medical records room. We were shown to an open cubicle, where a woman sat, clicking away on her computer. The woman said hello, and the nurse told us she'd be back in a bit to get us. After ten minutes of answering questions, signing papers, and scheduling my next few appointments, the nurse returned to get us. We left the room and went across the hall. The nurse scanned her badge, the doors to the nurse's area opened, and we stepped inside.

Deja vu, I thought, as once again my weight was recorded and my blood was drawn. After those tasks were completed, we returned to the waiting area. This time, I was told to wait in the other waiting area, the one I'd just noticed today. Meg and I spoke a little, tried to laugh and keep things calm, and waited. After a bit, we heard a click and the two large doors in front of us opened.

A Turning Point

A different nurse, wearing colorful blue, green, and yellow scrubs, came out and called my name. Meg and I stood up and made our way to the door. The nurse was friendly, said hello, then asked us to follow her. As we stepped inside, I felt the room's coolness and heard the doors click shut behind us. In front of us was a spacious room with pale orange-colored walls and wooden floors. In the middle of the room was a nurse's area, bustling with activity. On the outside of the room were small spaces partitioned off with white drapes. Inside each small room were one blueish-green reclining chair, a small blue chair, a small TV, a rolling doctor's stool, and a portable computer stand.

We turned left and walked down to the fifth small room on the right. The nurse handed me a hospital gown and quietly asked me to change out of my shirt and into the gown. As the nurse left, she closed the white curtain behind her, which made a quiet, yet high and shrill scraping noise as she did. Meg sat in the blue chair as I undressed and put the hospital gown on. I sat down on the blueish-green reclining chair, feeling the coolness of the material beneath me. The room had an odd odor to it. Not good, not bad, but noticeable. I could hear monitors beeping, people talking, and the low sounds of a nearby television. I was nervous and felt cold, but I mustered up as much positivity and friendliness as possible.

The nurse came back and told me what to expect. First, she would clean off my port. Then, she would put an IV in it. The IV would be hooked to my chemo cocktail, which would take a few hours to receive. She also told me that halfway through my treatment, she would administer one specific drug by hand. The drug, a deep red color, had to be given by hand because of its lethality. It needed to be administered carefully to ensure safety.

After a few hours, I was done. Meg's parents lived nearby, and we decided to stay with them for extra support. That night, we hung out, and I felt fine. I remember thinking, *This isn't too bad. I've got this.* The next morning, a Saturday, reality hit. I felt a level of exhaustion that I'd never felt before. I couldn't get out of bed. All I wanted to do was sleep; I was sick to my stomach. The nurses had warned me that if I started throwing up, I might not be able to stop and might need to go to the hospital for assistance. To help prevent this, I didn't eat, which was fine with my stomach.

I woke up Sunday morning and felt slightly better, but I was still really tired. I headed back to the hospital as my care plan called for me to receive a Neulasta shot. This shot, which needed to be administered twenty-four hours after chemo, helped my body produce white blood cells, an important part of the body's immune system.

After receiving the shot, we headed back to our house so I could rest. I realized that this was now a part of my life, my reality. The countdown began. One chemo down, five more to go.

Over the next ten weeks, my routine was the same. I'd get chemo every other Friday afternoon and return to the hospital for my Neulasta shot the following Sunday. I'd spend

Friday night, Saturday, and Sunday sleeping, feeling sick and exhausted. Monday, I'd get up and drag myself to work.

After the second round of chemo, my hair began falling out. The first time I noticed it, I had just gotten out of the shower and was brushing my hair. Suddenly, I saw a huge clump of hair fall into the bathroom sink. I knew then that I could no longer hide what was happening. I went to work that day and asked Tod to please let people at work know what was happening. I wanted privacy but knew it was time to tell those around me. I was flooded with love and support from my co-workers. One of many silver linings I'd receive amid my personal darkness.

As the chemo treatments stacked up, so did the effects. Halfway through my treatment plan, I had to stop working on Mondays. The level of exhaustion and sickness increased with each chemo treatment. I'd walk around the house in a daze and try anything and everything to help my stomach from hurting. Nothing worked. My sense of smell increased. My urine had a potent smell from all the chemo chemicals in my body. I would hold my breath while going to the bathroom and sprint out as soon as I could when finished. The smells of the chemotherapy area were intense and revolting. Each time I walked into the room, my body would immediately react, and I'd fight the urge to vomit. Life felt miserable. I hated looking in the mirror and seeing my bald head. I stopped going places and spent most of my time between work and home. I lived in a bubble. I felt shame for being sick and embarrassed with how I looked.

On the outside, I acted positive and as if everything was ok. I'd receive a weekly call from a mental health nurse. I always had the right answers to her questions. I didn't realize at the time that part of my soul was dying. The innocence of life was being torn away, creating a black hole inside me.

I did have something to look forward to—the golden bell. On the first day of my chemo treatments, I'd learned about the golden bell that hung prominently on the wall by the nurse's station. Upon finishing their last chemo treatment, patients would ring the bell to signify being done. It was always a celebrated moment. Every time I walked into the room, I'd look over at the bell and focus on the day I'd get to ring it.

It was the day of my last round of chemo, and I couldn't wait to ring the golden bell. After going through the usual routine, I gathered my stuff, stood, and began walking to the bell. As I did, all the nurses in the room stood and crowded around. I hugged my nurses, thanked them for my care, then reached up and rang the bell. The sound was beautiful, a symbol of triumph. I'd had my last chemo treatment, or so I'd thought.

Several weeks passed, and I was back in an examination room waiting to see Dr. Rothschild. I'd had some testing done, and the results were in. He walked in, holding my file. I was expecting to hear him give me the date to start radiation. Instead, he told me he'd looked at my test results and shared my case with several of his colleagues. Together, they recommended I do two more rounds of chemotherapy before starting radiation. Not only was I taken off guard by the recommendation, but I was also distraught.

A Turning Point

I rang the bell. I never thought I'd have to walk back into that room.

Dr. Rothschild was calm and understanding. He told me to think about it. If I chose not to do the additional rounds, I needed to start my radiation treatments immediately. I left the hospital, heading back to work, feeling scared.

I arrived at work in time for a meeting. I went into the empty conference room and sat down at the large, brown, rectangular table. I was dazed and confused. The conference room was cool and surrounded by large windows. I turned and saw my reflection. Looking back at me was someone I didn't love. A pang of disgust entered my mind. I hated what I was seeing, what I was feeling, and what I had to decide. A bald, white head and dull, lifeless, scared eyes stared back at me. Every bit of me hated the thought of doing more chemo. But how could I go against my doctor's recommendation? My body slumped forward, exhausted.

I pulled away from my thoughts as I heard Tod walk in and ask, "Trina, how did it go?" I turned my chair to face him and felt the lump in my throat grow. Behind him, a few of my closest co-workers walked into the room, anxious to hear. I replied, "My doctor recommends I do two more rounds of chemo before starting radiation." As the words flowed out of my mouth, tears began flowing from my eyes and down my cheeks.

That day was the day I decided to take control of my life.

Ironically, the company I worked for was a health and wellness company. I now truthfully joke that while I worked there, I didn't live nor understand the lifestyle they promoted. I knew I needed to make some changes. Together, with the help of my co-workers, I began learning about the body and the role of food and nutrition.

Admittedly, I was a fast-food-eating soda-drinking kind of girl. If I started to put on a bit of weight or binge on unhealthy foods over the weekend, I'd work out a bit harder or play an extra soccer game during the week. I thought being physically fit was the same as being healthy. Clearly, I was wrong. I learned fast food, soda, highly processed foods, sugar, artificial ingredients, and preservatives all lead to obesity and other chronic conditions, such as cancer. This summed up most of my diet and may have been a big reason I got sick.

I learned the importance of eating whole foods—fruits and vegetables that give our bodies anti-oxidants. Antioxidants are molecules that fight free radicals in your body. Free radicals are compounds that can cause harm if their levels become too high in your body. They're linked to multiple illnesses, including diabetes, heart disease, and cancer. As mentioned in the previous chapter, foods high in antioxidants are green-lights and should be consumed abundantly.

I wasn't going to be a victim. I started removing sugar from my diet and increased my fruit and vegetable intake. I stopped eating fast food, decreased the number of processed foods I consumed and began drinking more water. I learned to read food labels and make healthier choices. I changed my life around and went from barely living to thriving. I now love who I am inside and out.

Power Mom Action Step:

Turning my life and health around required understanding what changes I needed to make and a willingness to receive help from people I trusted. What changes would you like to make in your health, and who can you turn to for support? Pssst....if you're not sure, Tara and I are always here to help you.

CHAPTER 10

Become a Power Mom Private Investigator (PI)

Lake Worth, Florida, June 2005
Trina's First PI Store Visit

The sun was setting, painting the sky with orange, pink, purple, and blue hues. I pulled into the busy parking lot and located a parking space opposite the new neighborhood market. I grabbed my purse, ensuring my shopping list and cheat sheet were inside. It was time to implement what I'd been learning since my cancer diagnosis.

I'd never felt intimidated walking into a grocery store before, but today I could feel a hint of overwhelm and anxiety. The vast warehouse building with bright green signage loomed in front of me as I made my way through the parking lot. I walked through the first of two automatic store doors and saw a few rows of shopping carts to my right. I grabbed a cart and rolled it through the second set of doors. As I walked through, I felt a rush of chilly air blow over me from above and felt the coolness of the air inside. I stopped and looked

CRUSH MOM GUILT

around. Wide aisles flanked by shelves of food filled the space inside. The store was lit brightly, with white walls and green signs indicating what was within each row around the store's perimeter: Produce, Deli, Pizza, Bakery, Dairy, Fresh Meat, Pet Care, Paper & Cleaning, Health & Beauty, and Pharmacy.

I glanced at my cheat sheet and read the first tip. "Shop the store's perimeter first, and only step into the aisles when needed." *Easy enough*, I thought as I walked further into the store and turned right. In front of me, a large sign hung from the ceiling that read "Produce." Below the sign were bins of colorful fruits. Along the sides of the produce area were cold food cases full of vegetables. I checked my shopping list and started to fill my shopping cart with an array of fruits and veggies.

Next, I headed to the deli. I'm a sandwich-loving girl by heart, so I knew this store section would challenge me, as I was limiting foods with added nitrates—such as lunch meat, bacon, hot dogs, and other processed meats. They have added nitrates which prevent bacteria from growing and give the meats their pink color. The keywords I was watching for were added nitrates or nitrites, potassium nitrate, sodium nitrate, and cured or smoked.

Since I was reducing my deli meat intake, I'd created a list of foods to replace my meaty sandwiches.

- Peanut butter and honey sandwich
- Veggie plate with crackers and hummus
- Avocado sandwich
- Egg salad sandwich
- Loaded salads that included a variety of colorful veggies

I moved from the deli section into the dairy area. I grabbed some almond milk, a few yogurts, cheese, cottage cheese, and butter. I strolled into the meat section and grabbed ground beef and chicken. Now that I'd shopped most of the store's perimeter, it was time to pull out the cheat sheet again and look at the other tips.

Tip #1: Don't be fooled by the *big* letters on the front of the package. The front of the package is a commercial area designed to sell the product. Food companies know parents want their families to be healthy, so they make their foods look more healthful than they are. Instead, check out the nutrition facts label and ingredient list. You can find the *truth* on the back of the box. These details are written in small print, but they tell the whole story!

Tip #2: The *first* ingredient on the list is always the *biggest*! By law, ingredients on a food label must appear in a certain order. The first ingredient makes up the largest amount of the product by weight. The second ingredient has the next largest amount, and so on.

Tip #3: Avoid foods that contain sugars added during the manufacturing process. Most consumed sugar comes from sucrose, a combination of glucose and fructose, which makes table sugar. Food labels are confusing as food manufacturers attempt to hide added sugars. In other words, the manufacturers rename the sugars. For instance, you may find the word maltose on an ingredient label and never know it is an added sugar. You can do a Google search to find a full list of current sugar names.

Sugar is sugar, even if it occurs naturally, right? Yes, but context matters. When sugar enters your body, the digestive system views natural sugars and added sugars the same and processes them as such.

And while certain fruits and vegetables have sugar in them, they also contain fiber, vitamins, and minerals. Because of this, these foods are digested more slowly and leave you feeling full longer. You don't need to eat a lot of fruits and vegetables before being satisfied, which keeps the amount of sugar consumed in check.

Added sugars, on the other hand, contain no nutrients or dietary benefits to slow down digestion. This is why they're commonly referred to as empty calories. There's a reason you can eat sugary foods, such as several cookies, and not feel satisfied. So fill up on those green-light foods—fruits and veggies—and stay away from sugary, red-light foods.

Tip #4: Avoid foods that contain partially hydrogenated oil. Partially hydrogenated oil is a "transformed fat," also known as trans fat, made by changing healthy liquid oils into artificial saturated fat. Food makers like it because it tastes good and has a longer shelf life than healthy liquid oils. Trans fat raises cholesterol, contributes to heart disease, and encourages your body to store fat.

Tip #5: Fiber is your friend. It's good for your body and helps get nutrients from your food into your cells, allowing the cells to tell your brain, "I'm full!" It helps move food through the digestive system, and you stay full longer when you eat a meal high in fiber. Beware of whole-grain imposters. Choose loaves of bread, cereals, granola bars, crackers and pasta with at least two or more grams of fiber per serving. Whole foods high in fiber are black beans, avocados, figs, broccoli, brussels sprouts, sweet potatoes, pears, kidney beans, nectarines, carrots, apples, apricots, oats, flax seeds, and bananas.

After reading through the five tips, I checked ingredient lists and got the rest of the foods on my shopping list. It was a bit tedious, but I left the store feeling accomplished. I'd stuck to my list, made the best choices I could, and I was ready for the week. In the weeks following, I found my shopping time began to decrease. I was now clear on what foods to buy. I kept to the store's perimeter and only stepped into the aisle for certain items.

Cheryl, one of our VIP moms, shared how much fun she had with her daughter every time they went to the store. They turned the mundane shopping experience into one of learning, growth, and tons of laughter. Here is what she shared, "Elise and I love to read labels at the grocery store. It's amazing the big words they like to call unhealthy ingredients. We make it a game on who can find the healthiest item. We have two requirements. First is the least amount of ingredients. Second is the healthiest ingredients. Additionally, the ingredients must be words we can pronounce and identify. As we go through different products, we will state whether it's a red-, yellow-, or green-light. We make shopping fun."

Power Mom Action Step:

Go into your Power Mom Action Guide and locate your Power Mom PI cheat sheet. Snap a picture to keep in your phone, or place the list somewhere you can easily access whenever you're shopping. Keep it handy and use it with each food shopping trip. If you still need to download your Power Mom Action Guide, you can do so at: https://www.crushmomguilt.com/action

CHAPTER 11

Slay Excuses and Create Endless Motivation

Colorado Springs, Colorado, February 2012
Life Before Kids

The clock strikes five, and I'm on the move. After a long day at work, I'm ready to bust out of the office and begin my evening. I grab my coat and my work bag and head out to my car. The night air is cool and brisk. The sun is beginning to set behind Pikes Peak, the highest summit of the southern Front Range of the Rocky Mountains. The evening sky over Colorado Springs is dark purple and deep blue colors; the brightest stars are just beginning to show.

I get into my car, head out of the parking lot, and within a few minutes, I merge onto I-25 North and settle in for the drive ahead of me. Traffic is busy but moving at a decent speed. Twenty minutes later, I see a lighted green exit that reads Rockrimmon. As I drive underneath the sign, I move to the far-right lane and take the exit. I turn left, drive another few

Crush Mom Guilt

miles up the road and turn into the Safeway parking lot. I pass the Safeway and drive towards the back side of the parking lot to a string of smaller stores. I glance over to the windows painted with *Anytime Fitness* and notice a parking spot right in front of the door. Awesome! I park, turn off the car, grab my gym bag, and head toward the gym door. Flashing my key fob at the receiver hanging on the wall beside the door, the door clicks open, and I step inside.

The noisiness hits me first. Loud, upbeat music. Clanking and the thudding of weights. Grunts, slamming locker doors, and shouts over the background noise. The gym is busy and lively. In front of me are two rows of treadmills, stationary bikes, and ellipticals—all occupied. I step further into the gym. On my left is a small stretching area; on the right, the room expands to a large space full of exercise equipment. Further back on the left are the men's and women's locker rooms, and a group class is taking place in a spacious room just across the hall. The walls are lined with mirrors. I hear the aerobics instructor enthusiastically saying, "Thirty seconds left; you've got this!" Followed by "What can you do in that amount of time? Don't give up!" I smile to myself as I appreciate her enthusiasm. Now it is time to get myself changed and motivated.

As I walk into the locker room, I notice the clock on the wall says 5:25. Time to get moving. I find an empty locker and set my bag on the bench in front of it. I unzip my bag and pull out my workout clothes, water bottle, tennis shoes, earbuds, and iPhone. I put my car keys in a small pocket on the side of the bag. I change out of my work clothes and pull on my workout clothes. I put my work clothes and gym bag into the locker, then shut and lock it. I stop by the bathroom on the way out of the locker room. After washing my hands, I put my hair up and make sure I look good.

Ten minutes later, I'm finally ready. I head out to do cardio. All the treadmills and bikes are taken, so I opt to jump on the only open elliptical. I slip my earbuds in, choose my workout music list on my phone, and as the music vibrates in my ears, I hit start on the elliptical. After fifteen minutes, one of the treadmills opens up, so I decide to finish the last fifteen minutes of my cardio there. Out of breath, hot and sweaty, I hit the stop button on the treadmill. I step off and grab a towel off of the towel rack. After wiping sweat from my face, I take a long drink from my water bottle. *Ah…that hits the spot.* Next is upper body work, so I step over to the free weights area and roll out a yoga mat. A few other people are using the free weights, but thankfully I can grab the ten- and fifteen-pound weights. *I wish the twenty-pound weights were available, but I'll make do with what I have,* I think, as I set my weights down in front of my mat. I feel warm enough from my run, so I skip doing a warm-up and head straight into my workout.

- Bicep curl to overhead press—12 reps
- Overhead triceps extension—12 reps
- Alternating forward to lateral raise—12 reps
- Bent-over row—12 reps
- Glute bridge chest press—12 reps
- Burpees—12 reps

After doing three rounds of the exercises, I'm spent. It's already 6:40, and I'm ready to go home. I check my phone and see that Tara has sent me a text: "Meet me for Mexican at Salsa Brava?"

I replied, "Yes! I just finished my workout, so meet you in ten minutes." Luckily, the restaurant is in the same parking lot within walking distance. I quickly straighten up my weights and workout space and return to the locker room. After cleaning up a bit and fixing my hair again, I grab my workout bag and work clothes and drop them at the car. I'm starving and can't wait to split some chicken fajitas with Tara.

Montrose, Colorado, September 2022
Working Out as a Mom

My eyelids fly open as I feel the vibration on my wrist. It's 6:00 in the morning; time to get up. I turn off my watch alarm, roll out of bed, and quietly grab my phone, glasses, and water off the nightstand. I slip out of the bedroom and quietly shut the door, doing my best not to wake Tara.

To my left is the alarm keypad. I enter the password, turn off the house alarm and head down the hall to the bathroom. After brushing my teeth, drinking some water, and using the toilet, I grab the workout clothes I put out the night before and slip them on. I stop in the kitchen to turn on the coffee pot. As I walk out of the kitchen, I grab my earbuds, pop them in my ears and head into the family room. I plop down on the couch, take out my phone, select a meditation of choice and settle in. Twenty minutes later, I've completed my meditation and selected some upbeat music. Time to get my workout in.

I walk out the front door and head over to the shed we've turned into a workout space. The floor of the shed is covered with a black gym floor tarp. On the left side of the room is a free-standing mirror with a brown rectangular table next to the mirror. Sitting on top of the table, and leaning against the shed wall, is a black canvas with white block letters saying, "Life is Good." On the right side of the room is another free-standing mirror and a black shelving unit that holds five-, eight-, ten-, twelve-, fifteen- and twenty-pound dumbbells, two pairs of tennis shoes, a propane heater and a pair of gym gloves. The shed's walls remain in their original state; wooden two-by-fours spaced every sixteen inches placed to hold up the wall sheathing and siding.

In the middle of the room is a bright pink yoga mat rolled out, ready for use. I step inside, remove my shoes, and put my water bottle, phone, earbuds and glasses on top of the table. I turn and take a few steps over to the black shelving unit, where I grab the smaller pair of tennis shoes. After tying my shoes, I step back to my phone and click on the app to pull up one of our PM24 workouts. I put my earbuds in, hit play on the phone, and instantly hear Tara's voice as she instructs me what to do for the warm-up. Twenty-four quick minutes later, I'm hot and sweaty, ready to spend a few minutes stretching and then get back into the house to start my day. The kids will be up soon, and I want to spend a few minutes quietly with a cup of hot coffee. An hour into my day and I feel alive and full of energy.

It's Your Time

Mom life. It's true; free time just isn't what it used to be. It's one of the first things I realized when I became a mom. I now have these two adorable little beings who depend on Tara and me. The time I once had to do things for myself is now spent supporting my family and their needs. Leaving work, going straight to the gym, and spending hours with an impromptu dinner out is no longer an option. When Tara and I sat down and talked about what we needed to do to improve our lives, it was clear we needed to find ways to get our workouts in. So, we decided to start working out at home. Doing so has allowed us to feel good again, stay consistent, create time to take care of our family, and get our workouts in.

When I used to go to the gym, it took ninety minutes of my day. This included getting ready, driving to and from the gym, my workout and an additional few minutes for socializing.

Today, while working out from home, on average, I spend forty-five minutes a day. This includes getting ready, walking out to the shed, working out, stretching and walking back into the house.

Based on working out five days a week, I went from spending seven-and-a-half hours a week working out at a gym, to three-and-a-quarter hours a week working out from home. I cut my workout time in half. I've created a win/win for our family and me. I've created almost four hours of time to spend with my family. Yes, I could create time to go to the gym, but

I love working out at home and value my time. I also save on gas, and I don't pay for a gym membership.

I get it. Finding time to work out is hard, and getting to the gym can be a real challenge. Because, let's face it, making it to the gym is officially an event. Ninety minutes is precious time for a busy mom, so it's no wonder exercise stopped being a priority. But here's the deal, I do it, and so can you. There are a ton of different in-home exercises you can do that will save you time and get you results. If you don't already have a place to work out at home, create one. All you need is space, dumbbells, your water, and a great attitude! On the days you don't lift, find a way to incorporate movement. Bike, walk, rollerblade—do whatever you love to do, and stick with it. Doing something you love will help you stay consistent; consistency is key! Not only will you love yourself for it, but your kids will see what you are doing, and you will make a difference in their life and how they view staying fit and active.

We do recommend lifting weights a few times a week, and here are four benefits of doing so.

#1 Weight training builds muscle, and as lean muscle increases, your metabolism increases too—for up to twenty-four hours after a workout. The more intense your workout, the more calories you will burn.

#2 It strengthens your back, shoulders, and core, helping to correct bad posture, and prevent lower back pain. Additionally, eight training strengthens bones, increases bone density, and creates a healthy and strong spine.

#3 Weight training also increases strength in connective tissues, joints, ligaments, and tendons, preventing injury and relieving pain from osteoarthritis.

#4 Exercise and weight training release endorphins, which prevent pain, improve mood, fight depression, naturally reduce stress and anxiety, stimulate the mind, improve alertness and boost energy.

Simply put, weight training can brighten your entire day or help you combat a bad one.

One day, another VIP mom, Becky, reached out to us for help in overcoming her excuses. She was full of excuses for not being consistent with her workouts. Moms have some of the best excuses. Excuses are motivation killers. So, we broke down her excuses and challenged her to come up with two to three reasons for each one of her excuses. If you find yourself in the same excuse-making bucket, I suggest you take some time to do the same.

You see, you can have excuses, or you can have reasons. You can't have both. When you create reasons for doing something and keep your focus, the excuses fall by the wayside. The most difficult part of taking action is overcoming the excuses and focusing, instead, on your reasons. This arms you with the power to overcome negative thoughts or excuses when they pop into your mind. Switching your focus over to the action aligns you with reaching your goals. You will have to learn how to mentally prepare yourself and tell yourself every day that you can do it. Being prepared is key. Creating a mindset of making the right choice when you are in the moment of excuse-making or temptation is where the rubber meets the road. Making the right decision in those moments is when your strength and growth happen.

Here are the top three excuses we hear from moms and some solutions to each.

Excuse #1: I'm too tired to exercise.

Gosh, have you ever said this? You know, exercise is a funny thing. It can tire your muscles, but you get energy from doing it. Exercise increases blood flow, so your heart pumps oxygen to your brain, muscles, and tissues faster. It releases natural endorphins that make you feel better and more energized.

So, how do you overcome the I'm too tired excuse? Here are three solutions:

Solution A: I hate to break it to you, but when you're feeling too tired to work out, the solution is to go exercise. Work your inner strength and get yourself moving. You'll feel proud and rejuvenated afterward. Keep this saying in mind, "The first mile is a liar. Don't believe it." I've found this to be true. Some days, the beginning of any workout is the most difficult. Press past that level of discomfort, and everything will improve. You'll never regret a workout you've finished.

Solution B: Get a buddy. Exercising with a friend can motivate you to keep your commitment even when you are feeling tired. Keep each other accountable. You'll be grateful for one another.

Solution C: In our Power Mom VIP program, we strongly recommend working out first thing in the morning before your day gets away from you. Wake up thirty minutes earlier and move your body. You'll feel accomplished before the craziness of the day starts.

Excuse #2: I'm too old, fat, uncoordinated, or embarrassed to exercise.

When something is new and uncomfortable, avoidance is a natural response. You may feel too old, overweight, or uncomfortable in workout clothes. You may not know how to do a certain type of workout yet. Start small. It is essential to act and start with something. Here are two solutions to help you get started.

Solution A: If exercise is hard on your joints—for instance, your knees hurt when you run—then choose an exercise that puts less pressure on your knees, such as swimming, riding a bike, doing yoga, or Pilates.

Solution B: If you're self-conscious about your weight and don't want to be seen in your workout clothes, work out in the privacy of your home. We'll cover more about this in a bit.

Excuse #3: I don't have time.

Between kids, commuting, work, and other life responsibilities, your life leaves you feeling like there isn't enough time in the day to fit in a workout. Exercise becomes a low priority in your already crammed schedule. Here are three solutions.

Solution A: Instead of finding time to work out, make time. Look, some activity is better than none. The trick is to find a block of time in your daily schedule that is committed to working out. *Block the time*, and stick to it. Choose an exercise you enjoy. Want to re-ignite your inner athlete? Find an adult league in your sport of choice. Get those competitive juices flowing again. Not ready? Start walking or do a fun activity you enjoy and look forward to. Exercise doesn't have to be hard or forced.

Solution B: Exercise before you allow yourself to watch TV or scroll social media. How much of your time do television and social media eat up? On average, Americans spend over two hours a day on social media platforms. Train yourself to watch TV or get on social media after you've exercised. You'll likely find thirty minutes a day if you manage your TV and social media time.

Solution C: Work out at home. Get some weights, a treadmill, or a stationary bike, and get moving. Get your muscles working and your heart pumping with every workout. Within our Power Mom VIP program, our PM24 workout videos keep the guesswork out of what workout to do.

Consistent Action = Motivation

"How do you do it?"

"Do what?"

"How do you stay consistent with the Daily Practice, and what do I need to do to stay consistent too?" my friend Pam asks.

"I get asked this question often, and I'm glad you asked. The first step is to start. Sometimes moms get stuck before they even start. They begin questioning themselves, wondering if they are ready to commit, and the excuses take over. The excuses win; they freeze, do nothing, and stay stuck. So, take the first step and start. Make a plan. Write out what you want to focus on within each of the 4 Power Components and start."

Pam replies, "So, my problem isn't with starting, but rather staying at it. It's like a roller coaster ride of ups and downs from day to day. A while ago, I did really well with working out. I went three weeks in a row without missing a day in my routine. But then we went out of town, and when we got home, life started racing at me. I've not worked out since. This isn't the first time I've started and then stopped."

"You're right. Motivation only lasts for so long. Yes, motivational quotes, books, stories, and music are all great, but those things do not actually keep you motivated."

"So what keeps you motivated?" asks Pam.

"The secret is taking consistent action. I want you to remember this phrase anytime you start feeling stuck—motivation plus action equals motivation. For instance, when you take action, and you get your workout in, how do you feel afterward?"

"It always feels good."

Slay Excuses and Create Endless Motivation

"Right. So, when you take consistent action, those feel-good feelings build and stack on top of each other. Imagine being consistent for a few months instead of a few weeks. Do you think you'd start to see more results? How would it feel?" I ask.

Pam, laughing, replies, "Well, I don't know 'cause I've never experienced that before, but I'm sure I would lose some weight and feel proud for being consistent."

"Exactly. When you take that consistent action, you're consistently creating more motivation and momentum. You won't want to stop that momentum you've created and worked hard for. You'll fall in love with your results and want to keep working towards getting even more results. I've learned to fall in love with the process of taking consistent action, and the results always follow. This is the key to my consistent motivation. Everything Power Mom stands for is about creating a healthy lifestyle—taking steps to build habits that will last you a lifetime. It will get you off the roller coaster ride you've been on."

As Pam and I wrap up our conversation, I leave her with five tips.

1. Join forces with a friend, your partner, or a group of like-minded moms. Keep each other accountable. You're 40 percent more likely to fall into a routine and make working out a habit by doing this.
2. Write down how you feel after each workout.
3. Create for yourself a fun mini-challenge.

Crush Mom Guilt

4. Track your success.
5. Make your goals about times, distances, dumbbell weight, and reps, and *not* about how you look.

Power Mom Action Step:

What excuses do you make around exercising consistently? Here are two examples:

1. You're not clear on what consistent workout you're willing to do, so you use not knowing what to do as an excuse and choose to do nothing instead.
2. You have recorded, must-watch TV shows to get to, so you watch one to two hours of TV every night instead of working out.

Now that you're clear on your excuses, create a detailed, realistic plan you can follow and be consistent with. Here are two examples:

1. "I'll do the Power Mom 24 workouts in the morning four days a week. My workout days will be Tuesday, Wednesday, Saturday, and Sunday, starting at 6:30."
2. You know you're a snooze button lover, and you'll snooze past your 6:15 wakeup time which results in you missing your 6:30 workout time. So, set your alarm for 6:00, avoid the snooze button, and give yourself enough time to make your 6:30 workout.

Chapter 12

Everything Leads to This

Colorado Springs, Colorado, November 2015
911 What's Your Emergency

Twin life. It's been amazing to be a parent of twins. There is something special, a bit deeper, within their relationship. I mean, how could there not be? They've shared so much together since conception. Teegan is our little girl and twelve minutes older than her brother Tristan. Teegan is reserved, thoughtful, witty, and a ball of life in her own unique ways. Tristan is outgoing, helpful, full of wonder, and runs one hundred miles an hour from the moment he wakes until his head hits the pillow. The first year of their lives was a whirlwind. Admittedly, raising twins was a lot of hard work sprinkled with many joyful moments. What we didn't know during that first year was that life would take a turn we didn't see coming, and things would get a lot harder.

It was terrifying. I was standing at the kitchen sink doing dishes. The TV was on, playing kid's music. Tristan was behind me playing with Tupperware, while Teegan, in front of me, played in her bouncy seat. As I glanced up from the sink, I suddenly saw Teegan's head fall unnaturally forward, hitting the white tray of the bouncy seat. Her face was blue, and her entire body was shaking. I yelled, "No, no, no!" as I ran over to her and took her out of her bouncy. I immediately laid her down on the living room carpet. I thought she was choking, so I swept my finger in her mouth. The chattering of her teeth caused her to bite my finger, but I kept probing until it was clear nothing was inside. I grabbed my phone. My hands shook hard as I quickly dialed 911. Suddenly, I heard the dispatcher's voice, "911. Is this an emergency?"

"Yes!" I yelled. I quickly described what was happening. The dispatcher stayed calm as she asked me questions about the situation. She reassured me that the paramedics were on their way and she'd stay on the phone with me until they arrived. I don't clearly recall all the details, but during the length of the call, Teegan stopped shaking, and she began to breathe again. The paramedics finally showed up. As two paramedics attended to Teegan, a woman paramedic started asking me questions, going over the details I had just told the dispatcher. I called Tara, who was at work, quickly told her what happened, and asked her to meet us at the hospital. I called my neighbor, who came over immediately, and asked her to watch Tristan. Then, Teegan and I were whisked away in the ambulance, lights flashing, heading to the emergency room.

Unfortunately, this was the first of many grand mal seizures for Teegan. Over the next several years, Teegan underwent many tests and met with a wide variety of specialists.

Everything Leads to This

With each brain scan, the results came back the same; nothing was found wrong or abnormal. No one had any answers as to why she was having seizures. We put her on medication, which, thankfully, stopped the seizure activity. As we leaned more into Teegan's health, it became apparent something was wrong, even if we hadn't yet figured it out. Eventually, we learned about her diagnoses and found them to be complex. They include seizure disorder, learning disabilities, developmental delays, autism, and ataxia. Ataxia is a degenerative disease of the nervous system. It affects her coordination, balance, speech, eating, fine motor skills, walking, and running, and her body often tremors. She doesn't know life without therapy—physical therapy, occupational therapy, or hippotherapy, which uses horseback riding as rehabilitative treatment.

Because of all this, Teegan needs extra care and attention. Every activity in our lives considers her disabilities. We often pass up doing physical activities that kids her age typically can do or have to find special ways to adapt. For instance, at age eight, she can't yet ride a bike. We have a special seat for her that attaches to our bikes, so we can pull her along.

She needs special equipment. She learned to walk using a walker and needs assistance when her body gets tired and her endurance wanes. She has braces for her feet and wears a special SPIO vest for core compression. We help her with daily tasks such as getting dressed, brushing teeth, bathing, and walking up or down stairs.

Communicating with Teegan takes patience. She needs time to process what she has heard and how she wants to respond. Too many things happening at once can be overstimulating and upsetting. To make sure she has heard us and isn't using selective hearing, we ask, "Teegan, did you hear my question?"

We focus on her nutrition, doing what we can to support her body. We utilize shakes to get some foods and nutrients into her body that she is averse to eating. Her body has difficulty moving fecal matter through her intestines, making bowel movements a challenge. Over time, we've learned to add certain foods and a whole-food-based shake mix to her daily regimen, which helps promote regularity.

While we've faced many challenges and adapted, life with Teegan is also amazing. We get to spend a lot of time with her, and we hold hands often, which we love. She has a sensitive soul. She is smart, determined, happy, and gentle. She loves to read, learn, and run in the way that suits her body. She tells jokes, likes to draw in a way uniquely her own, and she has an amazing memory. She perfectly recites and acts out stories she has read.

She has taught and challenged our family so much, physically, mentally, and emotionally. We've learned the importance of incorporating the first three of the 4 Power Components— Building You, Training You, and Fueling You—so we can be the best versions of ourselves. Doing this allows us to focus on the final Power Component— Extending You—so Teegan and Tristan receive the best love and care we can give them.

Oprah Winfrey once said, "Your life is a journey of learning to love yourself first and then extending that love to others in every encounter." The greatest gift you can give to someone is love and happiness. When you're in a state of joy, happiness, or appreciation, you're fully connected to who you are. When you are in that state, those around you benefit.

We started this book talking about your 2.0 Version—who you want to become. We did this on purpose because it is such an important piece to you living your dream life. When you give to yourself and feel fulfilled, you have more to give to those you care about, and you'll make a bigger impact in this world. You'll become the change this world needs. That's what the fourth Power Component—Extending You—is all about; creating deeper connections with those around you and the ones you love.

Colorado Springs, Colorado, October 2020
Trina's Moment of Decision

At the moment, I had to choose. My day started with taking our Rat Terrier dogs, Tia and Tobi, for a walk. They were nine months old, new to our home, and new to taking walks. The walk had been enjoyable, the day bright, with blue skies and a slightly cool fall breeze. We were finishing the walk, rounding the corner to our house, when suddenly, two medium-sized dogs ran out from across the street, charging at Tia and Tobi.

As I turned to face the oncoming and fiercely barking dogs, I lost grip of Tobi's leash. She fled to my neighbor's yard and hid behind a small bush. As I watched Tobi run away, I quickly scooped Tia into my arms just as the fierce dogs halted in front of me, still barking. I ran to where Tobi was hiding and picked up her shaking little body.

Carrying both Tia and Tobi, I left my neighbor's yard and headed into our house. As I did, two trucks pulled into our driveway. In one was a contractor we'd hire to redo our fireplace, and in the other were workers coming to do some concrete work.

I hurried into the kitchen, where Tara was sitting, doing some work. I excitedly started telling her about the dog drama just as the doorbell rang. At the same time, Tristan rushed into the kitchen. I heard his sweet, excited six-year-old voice interrupt my story with, "Mom, look what I built!" He extended his hands out and gave me his carefully built Lego creation. He continued, "This is a battleship. Here are the windows, the guns, and look here, it's a secret trap door." He pushed a button, and a small door swung open.

At this moment, I had to choose. It seemed everything was happening at once, and my emotions were running high from the dog attack. And here, amid chaos, our little son simply wanted to show me what he'd been working on and built.

I've learned a fine line exists between Tristan respecting and waiting for us to finish our conversation and me crushing his little heart and excitement because I feel what I'm talking about is more important.

This was the decision I had to make. I could shush him and send him along his way. If I did, I'd send the message, "You and your little Lego creation aren't as important as my big adult conversation or problem." Or, I could show interest in him and what he'd made. If I did, I'd send the message, "You, your creation, and what you have to share are important to me."

Let's be honest. My first instinct was the first option, but I'd been working on being more present with my kids. So, in this instance, I stopped my conversation with Tara and listened to him. It only took him two minutes to excitedly tell me about his masterpiece. What that did for his little heart was way bigger and more important than continuing my story to Tara.

After he'd shared his story, I told Tara I'd finish mine in a second, and I answered the door.

I'd recently read a perspective, a question, that stuck with me. I want to share it with you. "If you don't take the time to stop and listen to your kids when they are young, what makes you think your kids will come to talk to you when they are teenagers and life is much tougher?"

You can apply this concept to any relationship. People want to be seen and heard. One of the greatest gifts you can give anyone is presence. One hour spent fully present with loved ones goes further than five hours spent with loved ones thinking about that upcoming meeting, your email, scrolling your phone, or worrying about your to-do list. When you are fully present with your kids or partner and give them your focus and energy, it deepens the bonds of love and connection between you and creates the vibrant relationships you want.

Invent fun and creative ways to build connections. Have a weekly game or movie night with the whole family. Have

CRUSH MOM GUILT

family dinners together several times a week and discuss how everyone's day went. Once a month, schedule time to have one-on-one date nights with each of your kids. Do something your kid loves and give them 100 percent of your attention. Make time for your partner. Create moments of conscious and intentional time. Do a puzzle together instead of flopping on the couch and vegging out to Netflix. It doesn't have to be a night out or expensive.

One of my favorites is to do weekly planning together. We set a consistent day and time for the whole family to get together and go over each other's calendars for the week. This opens up opportunities for communication and lets everyone know that they, and their schedules, are important.

Hugs, hugs, and more hugs! Have you been hugged today? Silly question, right? Well, when you give or receive a hug, your body's brain produces a kick of the feel-good hormone oxytocin. This hormone creates feelings of connection, bonding, and trust. As a bonus, the effects compound. The more oxytocin you release by being affectionate, the more you want to hug, touch, or hold hands. It will support meaningful relationships and your long-term personal well-being and overall health. Oxytocin lowers stress, heart rate, blood pressure, feelings of fear, and depression. It boosts the immune system, heart health, and happiness.

Family therapist Virginia Satir stated, "We need four hugs a day for survival. We need eight hugs a day for maintenance, and we need twelve hugs a day for growth." So, be a light in this world, spread your love and give hugs!

Here's an ah-ha moment Monica, a VIP Power Mom, experienced:

"Holy cow, working this program has made everything click. This whole process makes complete sense. I've wanted weight loss and sisterhood, but today I found that this is so much more. This is about personal growth and not feeling guilty for putting my happiness first. I feel like a brick has lifted off my shoulders. My confidence is growing, things are clearer, and I can't get rid of this smile. I had no idea that was possible."

As you grow and gain confidence, you'll fall in love with yourself again. You'll naturally extend that love out into the world, improving the quality of your life and others.

Power Mom Action Step:
1. Right now, go and hug someone.
2. Choose or create one to two deeper connection ideas for your family and implement them.

CHAPTER 13

Action Takers Reap the Benefits

Colorado Springs, Colorado, May 2021
Saying Yes Gave Back

The summer day was bright and warm. The kids had ventured outside to play, and I sat at my desk engrossed in some work. I heard the chime go off, letting me know a door had been opened. A moment later, I heard the faint sound of footsteps heading toward the office door. Tristan walked in and said, "Mom, will you go on a bike ride with me?"

At the moment, I was tempted to say no and ask him for a rain check. In my heart, I knew if I said no, the rain check would never happen. So instead of saying no, I said yes.

Together, we left my office and headed outside for our bikes. His smiling face and joyful energy said it all. I was glad I had said yes. We rode together for about forty-five minutes, and we had an amazing time. Because I said yes, the memories of that day will last a lifetime for us both.

I acted because I knew in my heart it was the right time, the right thing to do. I've learned that action-takers reap the benefits and rewards from saying yes.

Throughout this book, you've read stories that have taken you on a personal journey toward becoming a Power Mom. Congratulations! You deserve to feel proud for reading this entire book and taking each Power Mom Action Step.

You started with your *why*, because without it, you'll find it nearly impossible to stay focused and committed to your journey. You gave yourself permission to dig deep and go big!

You were then introduced to the 4 Power Mom Components and the Power Mom Daily Practice. You then created your own Power Mom Daily Practice within each Power Component. The next stop was creating your 2.0 Version—which defines who you want to become. How great did it feel to dream again?

You moved into Power Component #1: Building You. Here you created your personal Power Mom Hour and "me" time. How fun was that! You're now armed with the powerful tool of declarations and the energy this daily practice creates as you grow your confidence and work towards your 2.0 Version.

Power Component #2: Fueling You. You started off by challenging yourself to stop and take a hard look at your relationship with food. This was most likely an eye-opening self-assessment that has given you new, empowering insights. Our hope is that you take these insights and move forward with awareness and inspiration. And how are you doing with your water intake? How great do you feel, and what benefits are you reaping? Now that you understand how to gauge your water intake, you're harnessing the power of water and supporting your body better. Next, you learned about a simple yet effective method of food management—the green light, yellow light, red light system. I'll bet you have begun to use this in your own life and are teaching it to your kids too! And don't forget about the healthy snacks list inside your Power Mom Action Guide. If you still need to download your Power Mom Action Guide, you can do so at:

https://www.crushmomguilt.com/action

You also learned why I, Trina, am so passionate about helping moms lead healthier, more fulfilled lives. With this, I asked you to reflect on what changes you need to make in your life and who you can turn to for support. Know that Tara and I are here to help you.

Power Component #3: Training You. Inside this Power Component, we shared the mightiness of working out from home and the benefits of adding weights to your workouts. You addressed your excuses and created solutions for each. You learned the secret to staying motivated—motivation plus action equals motivation. You're now equipped with tools to help increase consistent action, and you created a detailed and realistic plan you can follow consistently.

Power Component #4: Extending You. Last but not least, you headed into the final Power Component. As Oprah Winfrey reminds us, "Your life is a journey of learning to love yourself first and then extending that love to others in every encounter." The greatest gift you can give to someone is love

CRUSH MOM GUILT

and happiness. People want to be seen and heard. You invented fun ways to build connection. You embraced the hug challenge and learned about the many benefits of giving a hug, including releasing the feel-good hormone oxytocin. The more oxytocin you release, the more you create connection, bonding, and trust.

Tara and I hit different crossroads in our lives that challenged us to decide and act so we could improve our lives. We've been down this path ourselves and seen what is ahead of you. We've already navigated the peaks and valleys and know what it takes to get through the ups and downs of this process. What you decide to do from this day forward is important to us and, hopefully, important to you. You have the chance right now to go out and create the life you want. You're meant to do great things in this world. You are loved, and you deserve to reach your 2.0 Version.

The most common question we get asked at this point is, "Can you help me implement what you've taught in this book and do some of this for me?" The answer is yes. We created Power Mom to help moms go from exhausted, unmotivated, and troubled with mom guilt to energized, confident, and strong. Our goal is to help you reach your 2.0 Version, all while saving time and hundreds, if not thousands, of dollars in the process. If creating the life you want is a priority and you're serious about investing time, money, and energy in creating your success, the best step is to book a call with us to see how we can help.

Action Takers Reap the Benefits

On this call, we'll talk about your dreams, why they are important to you, and what your 2.0 Version looks like. We'll put together a customized plan you can use to get started. If you're a fit and qualified to work with us, we'll talk about the next steps and what that will look like.

If you're ready to start and think you might want to work with us, book a call with our team at https://www.powermom.co/call. While this book can help you with many things, it can't talk to you, hold you accountable, and create a personalized plan for you and your life. That's the purpose of this call, and it may be one of the most powerful forty-five minutes you've ever gifted yourself. If you feel this book has been a good use of your time, this call will be even more helpful.

We're on a mission to empower and inspire greatness in you through our programs. We hope you'll be our next Power Mom. Ready to commit? We know two things about you if you're still reading this book. First, your life is important to you. If it weren't, you wouldn't have purchased this book and read or listened to it all the way to the end. Second, you're committed to this. You're the type of person that finishes what you start, which is why we know you have what it takes to reach your 2.0 Version. It's time you commit to yourself and your life. We don't want this to be another book you've read, felt inspired by, and then forgotten about. Now is the time for you to act and improve your life.

One of our favorite Martin Luther King quotes is, "Take the first step in faith. You don't have to see the whole staircase; take the first step." You'll never find the perfect time to

CRUSH MOM GUILT

take that first step. You'll have to take that step before you are ready, and you may definitely experience sacrifices along the way. This journey won't be easy, but who you become because of it will be worth it.

You can't reach your 2.0 Version if you don't get started. It's time to get started. Best of all, you don't have to do it alone. We are committed to helping you become strong and confident... all without mom guilt.

Much Love,
Trina + Tara

P.S.

If you found this book helpful, and especially if you've successfully implemented the content in these pages, please leave a review on Amazon, letting us know your story.

P.P.S. Your next step—book a call with our Power Mom team if you're ready to get started on your 2.0 Version and you'd like our help at https://www.powermom.co/call

Acknowledgments

If you'd told me in early 2022 that I'd be writing a book, I would have looked you straight in the eye and laughed. This book wasn't a thought nor a plan in my mind back then. Then one spring day, as I was doing yard work, I was listening to the book "Looking For Lovely" by Annie F. Downs. Something she said, a question she asked, spurred an immediate thought of *Trina, you're supposed to write a book.* So I want to thank, and jokingly blame, Annie F. Downs for the writing of this book. Seriously, I love your work, Annie, and I hope I can become half the writer and speaker you are. I have several of your books on repeat within my Audible app. If you haven't heard or read any of Annie's work, do yourself a favor, and check her out. She's fun, real, and clearly, inspiring. You can find her at Annie F. Downs

https://www.anniefdowns.com/
https://www.facebook.com/anniefdowns and
https://www.instagram.com/anniefdowns/

To my wife Tara, thank you on so many levels, most importantly for believing in me. When I finally shared I was meant to write this book, you didn't bat an eye, and you've been my biggest fan. Thank you for listening to me read aloud on countless occasions and for your insights, knowledge, and feedback. This book would not be possible without you. From supporting my early mornings, creating time and quiet space, to being there for me when I hit some hurdles—thank you. Your belief in us, in Power Mom, and our family, is a beautiful thing, and I'm forever thankful to and for you. I love you.

To my son Tristan, and my daughter, Teegan, thank you for making me a mom. Thank you for the support you've given me while writing this book and the time you gifted me to do so. I love you both so much, and I'm proud to be your mom.

I want to thank Chandler Bolt for creating https://selfpublishing.com and for your whole team. Your expertise, insight, and knowledge have been an anchor for me. A very special thank you to Brett Hilker, Self-Publishing Coach, for your guidance, patience and endless support. https://selfpublishing.com

This book would *not* be what it is today without my awesome editor Amy Colvin. I immediately knew I was meant to work with you when I read your feedback. Thank you for your hard work and dedication to us and this book. I'm so blessed that you understood me, my writing, and for sharing your beautiful soul with me. You are a light in this world, and I am so thankful for all you've done to direct, help, and support me. Check out all things Amy Colvin at

https://www.amycolvinwordsmith.com/ and

https://www.amypatteecolvin.com/

Thank you to Jody Price for taking the time to write and share your thoughts and perspectives on my cancer journey,

Acknowledgments

which we took together. I'm forever thankful to you and our friendship. I love you and your family.

Thank you, Katherine Lee, for the inspiration and direction you've offered me - unknowingly - through the years. To learn more about the Pure Hope Foundation and their vision to Strengthen Families and Restore Survivors of Sex Trafficking, visit: https://www.purehopefoundation.com/

To all the teammates I've had throughout the years, thank you for the sweat, fun, and memories. Each of you have left an imprint on my heart in your own, unique ways. Thank you.

To our Power Mom VIP's. We love you, we believe in you, and you help us be better for you. We're honored to serve you. Thank you for choosing us!

And last but not least, I want to thank everyone that has been a part of this book-writing journey—whether your role has been big or small. From messages and comments of belief and excitement to input and suggestions, I thank you from the depths of my heart. This book is for you.

Author Bio

Trina + Tara O'Brien are partners in life and business. Moms of boy/girl twins, together they've created Power Mom. They are educators, coaches, speakers, health and wellness enthusiasts, and "all things" sports lovers. Using the Power Mom 4 Power Components, they empower moms to be strong and confident . . . all without mom guilt.

Trina grew up in Southern California while, Tara was born and raised in Long Island, NY. From the fields of AYSO in Southern California and her team, *Orange Crush*, to the *Shooting Stars* of Plainview, Old Bethpage Soccer Club, at young ages, both Trina and Tara fell in love with soccer. West coast met East coast in South Florida, where both played collegiate soccer and, years later, became a couple. In soccer terms, they joke Tara is the power while Trina is the finesse, the perfect combination for success.

Tara played Division 1 Soccer in Boca Raton, Florida, at Florida Atlantic University. Over the course of her four years, she proved her skills as a strong forward by being her team's leading scorer. She received a Master's in Leadership, utilizing these strengths while working with Fortune 500 companies.

She is also a nationally certified massage therapist and wellness coach.

Trina played Division 2 soccer in Boca Raton, Florida, at Lynn University. Over her three years there, she and her team won a national championship and made two Final Four appearances. She received her Master's in Sports Management, is a nationally certified massage therapist, and is a wellness coach. Her experience working within the natural health industry and the events industry fuels Trina's love for healthy living, growing relationships, and entrepreneurial spirit.

They now reside in Montrose, Colorado, their little piece of heaven. Together with the twins, they enjoy outdoor adventures, Jeep rides, RVing, Mexican food, and spending time with their dogs. While they both love mowing the lawn, Tara dislikes surprises, while Trina thinks surprises are fun. And as for superpowers? Well, Tara would like to be invisible, while Trina would like to transform Tara from invisible to visible. Power and Finesse at its best.

Follow Trina + Tara at https://www.powermom.co/

URGENT PLEA!

Thank You For Reading My Book!
I really appreciate all of your feedback and
I love hearing what you have to say.

I need your input to make the next version of this
book and my future books better.

Please take two minutes now to leave a helpful review on
Amazon letting me know what you thought of the book:
YourWebdomain.com/review
Thanks so much!
Trina + Tara - Power Mom

selfpublishing.com

NOW IT'S YOUR TURN

Discover the EXACT 3-step blueprint you need to become a bestselling author in as little as 3 months.

Self-Publishing School helped me, and now I want them to help you with this FREE resource to begin outlining your book!
Even if you're busy, bad at writing, or don't know where to start,nyou CAN write a bestseller and build your best life. With tools and experience across a variety of niches and professions,nSelf-Publishing School is the only resource you need to take your book to the finish line!

DON'T WAIT

Say "YES" to becoming a bestseller:
https://selfpublishing.com/friend/

Follow the steps on the page to get a FREE resource to get started on your book and unlock a discount to get started with SelfPublishing.com

Made in United States
Orlando, FL
28 June 2023